Guidance for IT Asset Management

Table of contents

Preface

Today all organizations aim and aspire for optimum utilization of IT assets, cost reduction, elimination of wastage, effective asset tracking, and appropriate asset disposal mechanism as per the laws and regulations. But with limited resources and knowledge available on ITAM practice, many organizations are very desperately seeking for help, guidance, and directions for effective management of IT assets.

Many organizations and consultants are very interested to understand and implement ITAM practice and its processes. Professionals and students are enthusiastic to know the importance, differentiation between ITSM & ITAM, and benefits for IT department & organizations through ITAM.

While understanding the need, demand, and enthusiasm for ITAM from varying audiences (CXO's, IT managers, Operational managers, Analysts, and Students), this book has been designed in a very easily understandable approach through procedural instructions. This book doesn't only talk about the theoretical concepts (like overview of the ITAM practice, goals, benefits, and activities),but also provides overall view on ITAM processes, implementation steps for ITAM processes (Strategy generation for IT Assets, Financial Management for IT Assets, Asset Procurement, Asset Inventory, Asset Catalog Management, Software License Management, Asset operations and maintenance, Asset Disposal, Asset Reporting, Asset Auditing), guidance for designing workflows to ITAM tools, and details the checklists for management and operational teams (which can be helpful in evaluating the effectiveness of different ITAM processes and operations).

Guidance for IT Asset management is not a 'run on the mill' book with convoluted theoretical concepts which beats around the bush about same concepts. It aims at providing a concise and clear direction in a user friendly and understandable approach for all the ITAM audiences (newbie's, intermediates, and experts) and IT stakeholders.

Acknowledgments

My eyes established a vision for my life,

After seeing the beauty of Lord Shri Krishna (with belief, devotion and love).

My senses started working intelligently,

After understanding the morals of Lord Shri Krishna's stories and his past times (with belief, devotion and love).

My hands started writing good books,

After folding hands in front of Lord Shri Krishna (with belief, devotion and love).

Oh Lord Krishna, what am I without your blessing,

Oh Lord Krishna, your blessing is the reason for my breath, for my actions, for health, for prosperity, for peace and everything that I possess.

Hare Krishna Hare Krishna, Krishna Krishna Hare Hare,

Hare Rama Hare Rama, Rama Rama Hare Hare,

I am grateful and would express my sincere thanks to my lord Shri Krishna, who has blessed me by giving the knowledge, knowledgeable friends, colleagues, and strong IT experience in world's best conglomerates which helped me in writing this book. Without his mercy, help and will, I wouldn't have been able to write and publish this book.

I am very thankful to my spiritual alma mater ISKCON (International Society For Krishna Consciousness), His Divine Grace A.C. Bhaktivedanta Swami Srila Prabhupada (Founder and Acharya of ISKCON), His Grace Kalakanta Prabhu who is my spiritual guide.

My special thanks to my CEO Xiaogang Wei (Simon) for encouraging me to write books and also helping me in getting most of my certifications. Also my special thanks to Angel Berniz and Thomas Wells for editing, formatting and structuring the manuscript.

Big thanks and very much indebted to Servicemanagers.org for publishing my book with great confidence; even though, it's my second milestone in authoring IT books.

About the author

Kiran Kumar Pabbathi has worked for various companies in the IT industry which gave him detailed insight of ITAM, ITSM, and ITIL best practices. Currently, Kiran works as a Quality & Process manager in Shanghai Bizenit Information Technology, China (www.bizenit.com).

Kiran has had the privilege to work in different roles taking care of service desk operations, request fulfillment, incident management, sharepoint administration, project management, ITIL consulting and trainings, and ITAM Consulting.

Kiran is a certified professional in ITIL® Expert, PRINCE2® (Foundation and Practitioner), Six Sigma Green Belt, ISO/IEC20K – Foundation, Cloud Computing - Foundation, TMAP – Foundation (Test Management Professional), MCP in SharePoint 2003 Customizations, and MCTS in MS Project 2007.

His other authoring works include:

- "PDCA for ITIL – Metrics, CSFs and workflows for implementing ITIL practices" published by TSO, UK (ISBN 9780117082076) which gives a direction for implementing ITIL processes and designing ITSM solutions.
- "Charm of friendship" published by Pothi, India (ISBN 9789382715924) explaining the importance of friendship for children.

How to read this book

This book will help in understanding the IT Asset Management key processes, concepts and provides an easy approach to implement IT Asset management practice in a process based approach. I have designed this book in an easily understandable way through the Deming's cycle (Plan, Do, Check, Act). This book can be a good reference and provide great value for IT Managers and IT Asset Management consultants (especially for the people involved in planning, design, implementation, and improvement of the IT asset management operations).

This book details IT Asset Management in terms of 10 processes that are depicted in 4 stages: Plan, Do, Check, and Act as defined in Deming's cycle; the 11th process describes the different methods to improve asset management as a practice.

The following information describes each section:

Basic Concepts

This section describes the Terminology, Overview, and Objectives of the process.

Steps for Implementation

This section describes the step by step implementation of a process through Plan, Do, Check, Act stages:

The plan phase details the important activities that have to be performed before making any investments on the process development and implementation. Hence, process leads will present the business case, goals of the process, project plan, and organization structure to get the confidence and approval from HLM (Higher Level Management).

The develop phase details the important activities that will initiate design, development and implementation of a process. Here, process leads and other supporting roles would take active involvement in executing the process and its activities.

The check phase details the important activities that will monitor, verify, and validate the process implementation and daily ITAM operations.

The act phase details important activities that will give feedback and recommend different ways to improve process and ITAM operations.

Measures

This section describes the Key Performance Indicators (KPI's) and Best practices.

Checklists

This section highlights the action items that have to be maintained for effective management of different IT asset management processes.

Also this book summarizes some important concepts like additional ITAM processes, ITAM for SSB (Small Scale Businesses), Roles and Responsibilities in ITAM, Principles for Effective Asset Management, Criteria for tool selection, Asset Management Process Maturity Framework, Demarcation between ITSM and ITAM, Demarcation between Asset Management and Configuration Management.

Frequently asked questions

If I want to implement ITAM processes in an organization, what is the first process that I should start with?

ITAM is a business practice with a collection of processes and it is up to you to select the process that you want to improve with respect to the problem areas in your organization.

If your organization is not effective in tracking and stocking of assets, you can refer to the asset inventory management process and define/redefine the process for your asset inventory team.

If your organization doesn't have a procurement team or is working inefficiently, you could refer to the asset procurement process and define/redefine the process for your asset procurement team.

If your organization is having issues with asset disposal activities, you could refer to the asset disposal process and redefine the activities.

If I have to implement all of the processes in ITAM, what is the procedure?

You can read this book and it would give you a fair idea of how to do so. Also, you can see the section Asset management PMF (Process Maturity Framework) and follow the procedure or customize the procedures as per your feasibility.

How can I win the confidence of my CTO/CEO in a way that ITAM processes would help IT in my organization?

Please refer to the Plan section of every ITAM process in this book; it provides all details.

What kind of VOI, ROI and benefits can I see after ITAM processes implementation?

After the implementation of ITAM processes, you would see maturity, improvement, and clarity in requesting, purchasing, stocking, tracking, and disposal activities of every asset. Apart from it, you would have:

- Clearly documented policies and procedures.
- Demarcation of roles and responsibilities, based on a RACI matrix.
- And you will not have to waste time reinventing the wheel again and again.

How to implement an ITAM process?

This book provides detailed insight on implementation of different ITAM processes. You can refer to the chapters "Steps for implementing <respective process>".

How much does it cost to implement an ITAM process?

There is no protocol or magical calculator that can estimate the costs; it depends on the organization and how effective they want the process and its team to be developed.

Should I follow everything that is mentioned in ITAM practice?

ITAM is a practice for management of IT assets; best practices and good practices are a collection of successful ideas. Hence, you can customize it how you want as per your company's feasibility, cost allocation, resource allocation, etc.

Are there any standards for IT asset management?

ISO/IEC 19770 is the only international standard for Software Asset Management (SAM), and organizations can aim for ISO/IEC 19770.

Why this book?

This book answers many of the questions that arise in the minds of beginners, intermediaries, and experts in the ITAM domain. Furthermore, it was written to provide clear direction for implementing ITAM processes while considering questions that came from students and customers in ITIL, ITAM training sessions and workshops. This book clarifies various questions like:

- How does ITAM help organizations?
- Where and how should I start? What is the first process that I should start with? What are the prerequisites?
- What are the most essential ITAM processes for an organization?
- Should I implement all of the processes if I have to manage my IT assets in the organization?
- Is there a step-by-step approach for developing ITAM processes?
- What are the inputs, throughputs, outputs, and outcomes delivered from processes?

This book is going to address all these questions and provides an easy to understand approach on ITAM best practices.

Introduction to ITAM (IT Asset Management)

What is an Asset

Organization's financial investments or costs on any kind of resources (hardware, software, and people) are called Assets. Assets can be classified into two types: tangible assets and intangible assets.

Tangible Assets: Assets that can be perceived physically can be called as tangible assets. Tangible assets are generally associated with a specific financial value and they can be converted into cash at any point of time. Examples of tangible assets are machines, materials, lands, etc.

Intangible Assets: Assets that cannot be perceived physically can be called as intangible assets. Intangible assets may not be associated with a financial value at all times. Examples of intangible assets are knowledge, processes, people, etc.

What is ITAM

IT Asset Management (ITAM) is a business practice with the collection of processes, people, tools and activities that aids on effective, efficient management of IT assets.

Effective management of IT asset operations can be performed by defining a standardized process for asset management, which encompasses strategy and planning for assets investment, acquisition, tracking, control, optimization, reporting, disposal, and auditing measures.

ITAM defines a standardized lifecycle for the management of IT assets; its lifecycle stages can be depicted as request, procure, receive, stock, deploy (install/ move/ add/ change), refurbish, retire, and disposal.

ITAM enables the IT organization in providing cost effective investment on assets, effective utilization of resources, effective tracking and control, and elimination of waste (Inefficient management of IT assets in organization results in unnecessary and additional costs, time, and resources).

Key important processes involved in IT Asset Management are:

1. Strategy generation for IT Assets
2. Financial Management for IT Assets
3. Asset Procurement
4. Asset Inventory
5. Asset Catalog Management
6. Software License Management
7. Asset operations and maintenance
8. Asset Disposal
9. Asset Reporting
10. Asset Auditing

And one continuous improvement initiative:

11. Asset Management Improvement Initiative

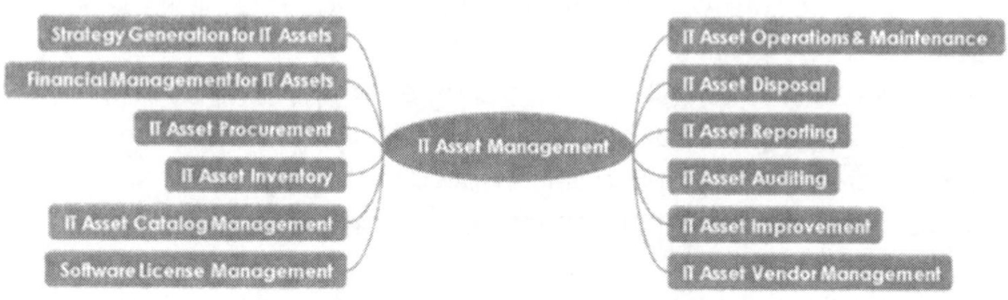

ITAM enables the IT organization to track and maintain accurate financial and technical information about IT assets throughout the lifecycle of an asset. Effective ITAM reduces the waste involved in the management of IT assets for an organization like:

1. Waiting time for assets
2. Unnecessary stocking of assets
3. Unnecessary movement of assets
4. Overproduction or over-ordering of assets
5. Unnecessary spending on assets

Why do we need ITAM

Lifecycle of IT assets, begins with requesting, procuring, identifying, stocking, tracking, auditing and disposing, and all of these activities are meticulously administered and managed by ITAM practice.

ITAM provides an appropriate direction for organizations, on optimum utilization of resources and reduction of costs on the IT assets. It provides an acute view on 'what assets organization has', 'where is it located', 'how are these assets utilized', 'whocontrols it', 'what is its financial value' and 'how to improve the utilization of assets'. Asset management helps organizations in various activities:

- To plan, control, manage, monitor, evaluate and provide accountability for IT Assets.
- To provide accurate asset information for various business processes.
- To provide real time visibility and status reporting on all IT assets.
- To make appropriate decisions on financial and compliance related areas like procuring and disposal activities.
- To develop single point of contact with accuracy and consolidated view on all IT assets.
- To track and monitor the costs of assets and pay the invoices on time.
- To register, track and monitor every IT Asset uniquely.
- To have better understanding on asset availability and reliability.
- To manage IT assets from requisition to retirement/disposal stage.
- To improve relationships with vendors and suppliers.
- To improve TCO (Total cost of ownership) while measuring all

aspects of an asset.

- To gain maximum ROI & VOI from the assets.
- To prevent the non-compliance issues on regulatory and contractual issues.

Scope of IT Asset Management

Many IT professionals and users often have a misunderstanding with the scope and activities involved in ITAM, as they presume that ITAM and ITSM (IT Service management) are the same. Scope of ITAM can be described as:

1. Asset requisition
2. Asset procurement
3. Asset costs tracking
4. Asset receiving
5. Asset inventory
6. Assets contract and license maintenance
7. Asset movement and maintenance
8. Asset retirement and disposal

Out of scope for IT Asset Management

1. Design or development of the assets.
2. Support and training activities on assets.
3. Associating relationship with assets and its associated configuration items.
4. Management of IT services in consideration with assets.

Goals of IT Asset Management (ITAM)

- Effective utilization and optimization of IT Assets
  ITAM provides accurate information of the assets, its location and status. It enables organizations to utilize and optimize the assets

appropriately and also enables in making accurate and effective decisions.

- Control assets as per the contracts agreed and signed
  ITAM provides complete control on assets with accurate and accessible information to improve transparency throughout the organizational stakeholders, and it feeds the audit systems to meet the contracts and compliance laws.

- Cost effective investment on assets, aligning to the business objectives
  ITAM helps organizations to achieve maximum return on investments and reduces the operating costs while satisfying the expectations and requirements of its stakeholders.

- Minimize the waste involved in management of IT assets
  Effective ITAM practice would eliminate wastage, reduce the capital expenses, risks, and deliver better customer satisfaction.

- Adherence to compliance and regulations
  Management of numerous assets, and its associated contracts would expose organizations to many risks on compliance and other regulations. ITAM practice can help organizations to ensure adherence with respect to compliance and regulations.

IT Asset lifecycle

IT asset lifecycle defines the series of stages that an asset transits from planning and purchasing stage to retirement and disposal stage.

IT Asset management lifecycle can be described through the following stages:

1. Plan
2. Purchase
3. Stock
4. Deploy
5. Dispose or Retire

Plan

Planning is the activity which communicates the organization's objectives and drives the execution of operations. In this phase, organizations define a plan with budget estimation, specifications, requirements, conditions, and stipulated time period for purchasing and stocking. Strategy generation for IT assets and Financial management for IT assets processes are greatly involved in the planning phase.

Purchase

As per the plans defined, organizations purchase assets ensuring they are economic in cost, good in quality, and that they meet the desired business objectives. Once the asset is purchased, it is associated with Financial management, Asset Inventory, Software License Management, and Asset disposal activities.

Asset procurement and Financial management for IT assets processes are primarily involved in the purchase of assets.

Stock

After the purchasing of assets, organizations stock the assets ensuring they are identified, categorized, and accounted to specific roles with specific responsibilities. Asset inventory process is primarily involved in the stocking of assets.

Deploy

Deployment of the assets is primarily handled by teams like operations management team (as defined in ITIL) which performs activities like IMAC (Installation, Movement, Addition, and Changes).

Retirement and Disposal

When an asset reaches the EOL (End of Life) period, the asset is either retired or disposed to ensure that the EOL asset doesn't disrupt any live services. Asset disposal activities should be done meticulously with adherence to environmental regulations and country laws.

Asset disposal process is primarily involved in retirement and disposal activities.

Strategy Generation for IT Assets

Introduction to Strategy Generation for IT Assets

Terminology

Asset: Organization's financial investment or costs on any capability or resource.

Strategy: Objectives and direction which lays the foundation for an organization to run its business and operations.

Capability: Any financial costs or investments made on intangible benefits like knowledge, process, etc.

Resources: Any financial costs or investments made on tangible benefits like hardware, software, etc.

Policy: Policies are management directives which significantly influence the processes and procedures.

Standard: Standards are rules and conventions that help implement policies and enforce required conventions.

Process: Process is a set or sequence of activities that results/achieves an output or business goal.

Best Practices: Practices that are well recognized and which have proved the ability for demonstrating success in respective areas, e.g. PMBOK for Project Management, ITIL for IT Service Management, MOF for IT Service Management, COBIT for IT Governance, etc.

Critical Success Factors (CSF): Critical success factors are the vital elements necessary for the success of business operations.

Metrics: Measurements which quantitatively evaluate the performance of IT operations.

Key Performance Indicators: The most important metrics which represent the performance of business operations.

Asset management policy: Foundational element for the ITAM practice which sets the direction for the IT asset management staff to perform different activities like managing and controlling the IT assets.

Asset management plan: Document which provides the holistic guidance on management of assets and its lifecycle. It provides an overview on service levels, risks, assumptions, roles, etc.

Vision statement: Statement that defines the organization's aspirations for future. It mentions "what do we aim for?" and "when do we want to do it".

Mission statement: Statement that gives an overview of the organization's purpose, organization's business, customers, etc. It mentions "what do we do?", "how do we do?", and "how are we unique?"

Overview

Strategy generation for IT assets defines a standardized process and procedure for defining the strategies with respect to acquisition and management of IT assets. It enables developing vision, objectives, critical success factors, roles and responsibilities, policies, plans and standards for the effective management of assets.

IT Asset strategy generation outlines and develops strategy in consideration with the business needs, profitability, risks, capabilities, resources, demand, costs, priority, technological and other factors. IT Asset strategy generation also helps in making decisions about investments as per business needs. IT Asset strategy generation builds the top level strategic plan that provides the foundation for subsequent planning in the management of IT assets with respect to costs, risks, and maintenance.

Important considerations for developing asset strategy are:

1. Identification of business needs and customer requirements
2. Definition of asset portfolio
3. Risk analysis
4. Cost and benefit analysis

Development of IT asset strategy is based on the IT Strategies and Organizational Strategies. Main deliverables of strategy generation for ITAM are:

- Asset management policy
- Asset management plan
- Vision and mission statement
- Service requirements
- Demand estimation analysis
- Risk assessment results
- Asset optimization model

Objectives

1. Develop strategy to manage the IT assets which will create value for the organization.
2. Identify the risks and issues associated.

Steps for implementing IT Asset Strategy

Prerequisite:

- IT Strategy, Organizational Strategy, Identification of business needs

Plan

Prepare the Project Charter consisting of Business case, Goal statement, Project Plan, Roles and Responsibilities.

1. Business Case
   Business case should describe the benefits and opportunities of IT Asset Strategy considering the following areas:
   a) Business needs of IT Asset Strategy.
   b) Who will lead it, and which department will control this project?
   c) What are the short term and long term benefits of this project?
   d) What impacts will this new initiative have on other business units and employees? (Pros and Cons)
   e) What are the risks and issues involved, what are the dependencies?
   f) Monitoring and Evaluation mechanism
   g) Cost and Benefit analysis

2. Goal statement
   Goals statement should define the goals associated with IT Strategy. Goals should be closely associated with Business case prepared. Goals should be SMART (Specific, Measurable, Achievable, Relevant, Time-bound). Goal statement should:
   a) Define the critical success factors?
   b) Define the key performance indicators?
   c) Define what is the time estimated to see the results?

3. Project Plan

   Project plan should show the timeline and milestones for various activities involved in the development of IT asset strategy.

4. Roles and Responsibilities

   Define RACI model for clarity in roles and responsibilities. Identify the roles needed and hire the human resources. Primary roles needed for IT Asset Strategy can be defined as:
   a) Asset Strategy Lead
   b) Strategy Analysts

Do

1. Develop the SOW for IT asset strategy, defining the:
   a) Scope of services which will be considered by IT asset strategy.
   b) Out of scope
   c) Hardware, Software, People-ware and tools required
   d) Appropriate people for the defined roles and responsibilities
   e) Risks and dependencies for the IT asset strategy team and process
   f) Costs Involved
2. Adopt Porter's five force analysis, Value chain analysis, and SWOT analysis to define a strategy suitable for the management of IT assets.
3. Develop vision statement, objectives, critical success factors, key performance indicators, metrics and roles and responsibilities (RACI matrix).
4. Develop policies and standards.
5. Develop the relevant planning documents like asset management plan, asset portfolio plan, asset maintenance plan, and other management plans like communication plan, improvement plan, etc.
6. Define classification schema for assets (into groups and hierarchy).
7. Develop Metrics and KPI's.
8. Perform technical and editorial review on the developed collaterals.

9. Document the feedback and comments on collaterals.
10. Ensure that the feedback is updated on the collaterals.
11. Publish and release the strategic collaterals.

Check

1. Ensure that developed strategy collaterals are in sync with IT goals and business goals.
2. Identify the risks related to each of the planned objectives, vision, and goals.
3. Review and update strategic plans and objectives as per changing business plans and requirements.

Act

1. Publish and release the strategic collaterals.
2. Maintain and store the developed strategic collaterals.
3. Review and update strategic plans and objectives as per the business plans.
4. Develop a continuous improvement initiative to identify and resolve any issues or flaws found in the strategic collaterals.
5. Develop plans to mitigate significant risks.

Measures

Key Performance Indicators

a) Number of plans defined.
b) Number of templates defined.
c) Number of policies defined.
d) Number of standards defined.
e) Time taken to develop the strategic collaterals (vision statement, objectives, CSF, etc.).
f) Number of human resources needed for developing strategy.

Best Practices

a) Develop strategy with clarity and concreteness.
b) Develop strategy aligning to the business needs and customer needs.
c) Explore the ongoing industry and technological insights to create a value for the business.
d) Development of strategy should be developed with the focus on end-user/customer's satisfaction.
e) Perform a SWOT analysis after defining the strategy.
f) Centralized and integrated asset management tool encompassing all the ITAM processes.
g) Active participation and commitment from the senior managers and executives.
h) Clarity in Roles and Responsibilities.

Strategy Generation for IT Assets Workflow

Analyze & Assess

An understanding is developed about the business requirements, patterns, organizational strategy, vision, goals and priorities. Assessments and analysis is made on market spaces, customer needs, types of customers (internal customers, external customers, and mixed customers), and risks associated.

Assessments are made in form of: Interviews, Questionnaire, Direct observation, Simulations, etc.

Define

Definition of strategy is done adopting Porter's five force analysis, Value chain analysis, and SWOT analysis. It defines strategic values like quality standards to be maintained, cost spending approach, utilization of resources, and considerations on warranty. It defines strategy as a closed-loop control system that can adapt to the changes and feedback provided.

Definition of strategy can be evaluated through methods like Brainstorming, Nominal group technique, Delphi technique, Multi-voting, etc.

Execute

It is the process of informing, implementing, and publishing defined mission, objectives, goals, and critical success factors for its stakeholders. Strategy execution has to be implemented into the most important artifacts like processes, products/tools, and people (internal and external).

Checklist for Strategy Generation for IT Assets

An effective strategy generation team should maintain the following data on its processes and operations:

Management's perspective

a) Is your IT assets strategy aligned with your organization's business needs?
b) Do you have the strategic goals, objectives, vision, critical success factors clearly documented?
c) Is the IT Assets strategy developed with the active involvement of key stakeholders and partners?
d) Are your customer requirements and competitors approach considered, while developing the strategy?
e) Are the emerging technologies and trends considered while developing strategies?
f) Is your previous learning's and experiences considered while developing the strategy?
g) Did you evaluate the risks associated with strategies?
h) Do you have an estimated time frame for the strategic goals and objectives?
i) Do you periodically review the strategy collaterals?
j) Do you have the roles and responsibilities clearly defined like a RACI matrix?
k) Is there appropriate segregation of duties in the RACI defined?

Operations perspective

a) Do you have the strategic collateral (objectives, goals, vision and etc.) accessible for yourself?
b) Are your internal teams and tasks adhering to the strategic plans as defined?

c) Do you know and understand your organization's strategic goals for the fiscal year?
d) Do you see the strategic execution in your company? Or do you think strategies are only made and never implemented in operations?

Financial Management for IT Assets

Introduction to Financial Management for IT Assets

Terminology

Budgeting: Forecasting and allocation of costs and investments to be made in an organization for a fiscal year.

Accounting: Statement or record that provides justification of the costs spent on different internal elements of a service or an asset.

Fixed Asset: Investments made on any tangible assets for long term use, and which will not be converted into cash in the planned 1-2 years.

Current Asset: Assets that are expected to be converted into cash or that will be consumed in the planned fiscal year. Current assets can be categorized into two types: Tangible and Intangible assets. Examples of tangible assets are servers, projectors, etc. Examples of intangible assets are contracts, copyrights, warranty, insurance, etc.

Fixed Asset Register: An accounting method that tracks and controls fixed assets, and also prevents misappropriation of assets.

Invoice: Document issued by a seller to its buyer or customer with complete details of the purchase, which includes details of the assets purchased, quantity, cost, taxes, insurance, etc.

Fixed Asset Reconciliation: Reconciliation of the fixed asset records in the balance sheets with accuracy to make effective business decisions ensuring there are no discrepancies.

Book Value: The value of an asset on a balance sheet for the fiscal year; It equals the cost minus accumulated depreciation.

Residual Value: Worth or value of an asset at the end of its useful life.

Depreciation: Decreased value of an asset, after a particular time period.

Asset lifecycle costing: An activity which determines the sum of all costs associated with an asset considering all the different stages of an asset like buying, deployment, operation, and maintenance.

Overview

Financial management for IT assets defines a standardized process and procedures for tracking and managing the financial aspects of an IT asset, throughout the asset lifecycle. It is responsible for different financial aspects of the asset management organization. Its primary responsibilities are:

1. Budgeting
2. Accounting
3. Invoicing
4. Fixed Assets Reconciliation
5. Current Assets Reconciliation
6. Intangible Assets Reconciliation

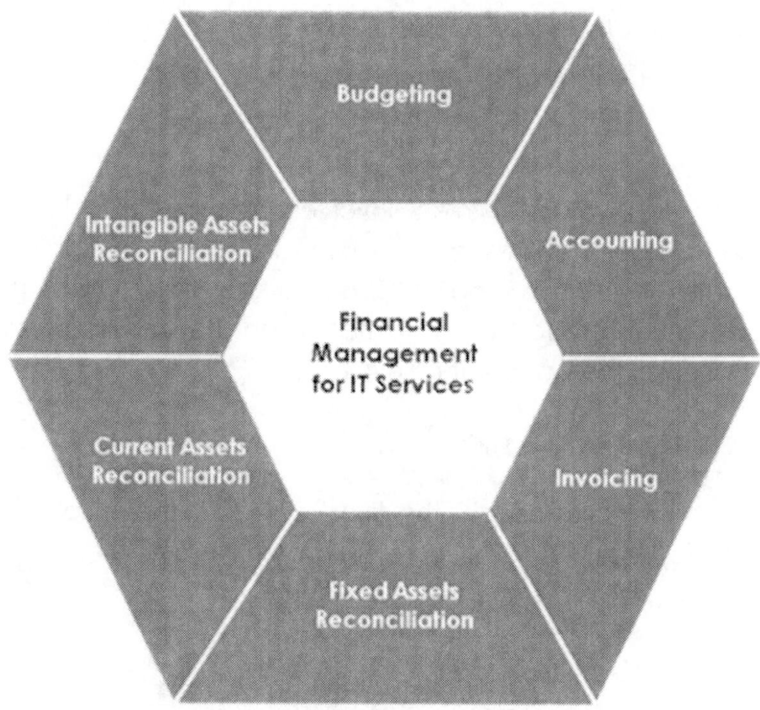

Budgeting

Budgeting involves planning, forecasting the expenses and allocation of money to different processes in ITAM. Budgeting would primarily focus on 3 areas:

- Run the ITAM: It is the budget allocated for operational activities on IT assets.
- Grow the ITAM: It is the budget allocated for introducing new assets.
- Transform the ITAM: It is the budget allocated for research and development activities.

Accounting

Statement that tracks, records and provides justification on the costs associated with an asset, following the rules and standards in GAAP and IFRS. Also it tracks, analyzes, and reports the variances between forecasts and actual expenses.

Invoicing

Management of invoices, which involves tracking the invoices, verifying the invoices with respect to purchase orders, and clearing payments to the vendors or suppliers. The invoicing team works closely with the asset inventory to get confirmation on the validity of assets received and gives the payment of invoices.

Fixed Assets Reconciliation

Fixed asset reconciliation tracks the fixed assets debits, book value, credits, and depreciation value to quickly reconcile the balance sheets and make effective business decisions.

Current Assets Reconciliation

Reconciles the current assets value in the balance sheets while enabling it to make wise business decisions.

Main deliverables from financial management for IT assets are:

- Cost models
- Budgeting, Accounting and Charging plan

Objectives

1. Calculate the monetary value of assets, throughout the lifecycle.
2. Assist in decision making of investments.
3. Maintain a database and track all the financial details in association with the assets.
4. Minimize unnecessary costs.
5. Ensure that the organization runs the business in accordance with financial compliance requirements.

Steps for implementing Financial Management for IT Assets

Prerequisite

- Defined Asset Strategy

Plan

Prepare the Project Charter consisting Business case, Goal statement, Project Plan, and Roles and Responsibilities.

1. Business Case
   Business case should describe the benefits and opportunities of financial management considering the following areas:
   a) What are the short term and long term benefits of this project?
   b) Does this new initiative align with other business processes, if anything exists?
   c) What impacts will this new initiative have on other business units and employees? Pros and Cons.
   d) Business needs.
   e) What are the risks and issues involved, what are the dependencies?
   f) Estimations on cost infrastructure assets and other miscellaneous items (hardware, software, people-ware).
2. Goal statement
   Goals should be closely associated with the business case prepared. Goals should be SMART (Specific, Measurable, Achievable, Relevant, Time-bound).
   a) What are the critical success factors?
   b) What are the key performance indicators?
   c) What is the time estimated to see the results?
3. Project Interfaces
   Define the boundaries, scope, relationships of the financial management.

4. Project Plan

   Project plan should show the timeline and milestones for various activities to establish financial management process in place and run the business.

5. Roles and Responsibilities

   Define RACI model for clarity in roles and responsibilities. Identify the roles needed and hire the human resources. Primary roles needed for Financial Management for IT Assets, can be defined as:

   a) Financial Lead
   b) Financial Analyst

Develop

1. Develop the SOW for Financial management process by defining the:
   a) Scope of services/service assets
   b) Services that are out of scope
   c) Appropriate people for the defined the roles and responsibilities
   d) Hardware, software and tools required
   e) Auditing frequency
   f) Costs Involved
2. Define standards for policies.
3. Define the policies for activities like budgeting, accounting, invoicing, etc.
4. Establish a database for tracking budget and costs associated with assets, accounting details, invoicing details, and auditing details.
5. Define a budget for all assets, comprising software, hardware, facility assets, compliance requirements, etc.
6. Define an invoice payment mechanism to capture the details of the invoices (invoice number, vendor name, invoice date and time, purchase order number, invoice items, quantity, unit price, total price and etc) and payments.

7. Perform accounting on fixed assets, current assets and intangible assets.
8. Develop depreciation calculation procedure for all hardware and software assets.
9. Consolidate asset values and replacement costs.
10. Define Metrics.

Check

1. Review the defined policies and standards.
2. Review the planned budgets with the cost spent.
3. Ensure all budget plans get approved by the financial lead.
4. Ensure all invoices are reviewed thoroughly with respect to purchase orders.
5. Resolve the discrepancies found in invoicing with the supplier.
6. Ensure all account statements are reviewed and approved by the financial lead.
7. Check the book value for all assets at defined regular intervals.
8. Ensure all financial transactions are stored in the respective databases regularly and accurately.
9. Keep an eye on asset amortization.
10. Ensure payments are done only for original invoices.
11. Ensure all fixed asset costs are recorded.
12. Depreciation charges are accurately calculated and recorded.
13. Perform internal audits at regular intervals to maintain the compliance.

Act

1. Up-to-date maintenance of all financial transactions.
2. Timely payments for the invoices.
3. Report the chargeback charges.
4. Inform all key stakeholders by producing periodic reports on:

   a) Costs on all assets
   b) Investments
   c) Return on investments
5. Perform financial audits.

Measures

Key Performance Indicators

a) Capital expenditure (Capex).
b) Operational expenditure (Opex).
c) Return on capital employed.
d) Net cash flow (which can be calculated by subtracting cash inflows with outflows).
e) Backlog volume of payments.
f) Budget adherence.
g) Compliance adherence.
h) Number of issues/discrepancies found in audits.

Best Practices

a) Prepare business cases for all investments, including the cost recovery mechanism.
b) Centralized budgeting for all assets.
c) Plan your financial strategy addressing every stage of asset lifecycle.
d) Adherence to the budget while allocating money to the departments.
e) Track all budget, accounting, invoicing transactions into the database in an up to date fashion.
f) Centralized and integrated asset management tool encompassing all the ITAM processes.
g) Documentation of all lessons learned.
h) Clarity in Roles and Responsibilities.
i) 100% Compliance adherence.

Financial Management for IT Assets Workflow

Investment Analysis

Investments on different assets are analyzed using variable cost dynamics (VCD) and investment analysis (IA).

- Variable Cost Dynamics (VCD) to analyze and understand the multitude of variables that impact assets costs.
- Investment Analysis (IA) to understand the costs on assets, licenses and expected return on investment and value creation (tangible and intangible).

Financial lead takes the accountability of financial Management process, policies, and standards. It also includes selecting the financial management tools.

Budgeting

This stage involves predicting and allocating the funds for all asset management processes. Budgeting is a proactive approach for investing and spending organization's money on various assets and processes. Budgeting activities are very reliant on IT governance and ITAM strategies.

Mandatory details needed for the budgeting phase are:

- Budgeted amount for a fiscal year
- Financial year
- Budget debit

- Budget credit
- Actual Spent
- Variance
- Date and Time
- Assigned to
- Expenses
- Total amount
- Currency type

Accounting

Accounting enables the financial management process to account for the way money is spent; it will allow identification of the money spent on different elements and its justification with reasons.

Accounting is done on different costs and investments like direct and indirect costs, capital and operational costs, fixed and variable costs, etc. Accounting is the activity that tells the financial management function about justification and reasons on spending and investments. Important considerations to be made while accounting are:

- Tracking of every expense, including the smallest spending.
- Maintenance of detailed descriptions for different spending.

Mandatory details needed for accounting phase are:

- Vendor's name and Contact
- Date and Time
- Quantity
- Unit Price
- Total amount spent on a manufacturer
- Original purchase cost
- Depreciated cost
- Replacement costs
- Market value (optional)

- Contact name
- Currency Type
- Billing address
- Tax
- Discount %
- Payment method, Payment terms and Shipping terms
- Status (Open, Paid, Invoiced)

Invoicing

Invoicing gives the assurance of selling and buying an asset as per the terms and conditions of the organizations.

Invoice is a document issued by a seller to its buyer; it describes the assets sold or purchased with complete details of the purchase including number of assets purchased, date of purchase, cost details, discounts, taxes, and delivery & payment terms.

Mandatory details needed for the invoicing phase are:

- Invoice description
- Vendor's name and contact name
- Date and time
- Quantity
- Unit price
- Total amount
- Approval code
- Status (Open, Paid, Invoiced)
- Discount
- Pricing scheme
- Tax

Audit

Audit verifies and validates the financial statements of a service provider/organization to check if the financial function operations are staying in sync with policies and procedures defined.

Financial audit helps to add credibility to the organization's management in that its financial statements fairly represent the organization's performance in terms of costs, investments, revenues, and profits, etc.

Auditing can be categorized into two types: Internal audit and External Audit.

An internal audit is the verification and validation of financial processes, policies, statements, reports and operations which are done by the internal stakeholders; an external audit is performed by the external vendors.

Checklist for Financial Management for IT Assets

An effective financial management team should maintain the following data on its processes and operations:

Management's perspective

a) Do you have policies for budgeting, accounting & charging, are they kept up to date, and are they communicated to the appropriate stakeholders?
b) Do you have procedures to ensure that all transactions are recorded in accordance with GAAP?
c) Is access to your financial applications limited to the privileged stakeholders in the organization?
d) Are your fixed asset records stored safely with backup copies (hard copy and soft copy)?
e) Do you have policies defined for the payments to suppliers and other stakeholders?
f) Do you have penalization policies defined for your suppliers?
g) Do you have enough budgets or funding allocated to maintain the assets?
h) Do you have the roles and responsibilities clearly defined like a RACI matrix?
i) Is there appropriate segregation of duties in the RACI defined?
j) Do you maintain centralized purchasing information?

Operations perspective

a) Do you follow the policies and standards defined?
b) Do you track all initial values or costs of all assets?
c) Do you track all types of payments on procuring assets like Initial payments, Easy Monthly Installment payments, Down payments, etc?
d) Do you track all purchased date, leased date details?

e) Do you track all monthly operating costs and total monthly costs?
f) Do you track total quarterly, bi-annual, and annual costs?
g) Do you track the budget spent in every month?
h) Do you track the current value of assets monthly or quarterly?
i) Do you track all direct and indirect expenses associated with assets?
j) How often do you audit your financial operations?

IT Asset Procurement Management

Introduction to Asset Procurement Management

Terminology

Procurement: The act of buying or procuring assets/services from a third party organization at economic costs.

Procurement cycle: A sequence of activities that are involved in procuring an asset.

Order: A formal instruction from the buyer to a supplier, requesting delivery of assets.

Purchase Request: A document created by the department or a team member mentioning the need and description of an asset, timeframe, and quantity.

Purchase Order: A document that is sent by a procurement team to the supplier to order the IT assets needed by an organization.

Request for Quotation (RFQ): A document prepared by a buyer inviting its suppliers to bid on its services/assets.

Request for Information (RFI): A document prepared by a buyer asking its suppliers to provide information about their services/assets and terms and conditions.

Request for Proposal (RFP): A document prepared by a buyer (who wants to buy an asset or service) asking its suppliers to submit business proposals.

Blanket Order: A purchase request that specifies to purchase a quantity of assets at a specific time, but doesn't specify the precise dates for shipments.

Lead time: Amount of time required to place the asset in operational usage from the time it is ordered.

Overview

Asset procurement management defines a standardized process and procedures for purchasing the assets in an organization. Asset procurement acquires the assets at best possible cost without compromising quality and utility. A holistic picture of asset procurement activities can be described by the sequence of below activities:

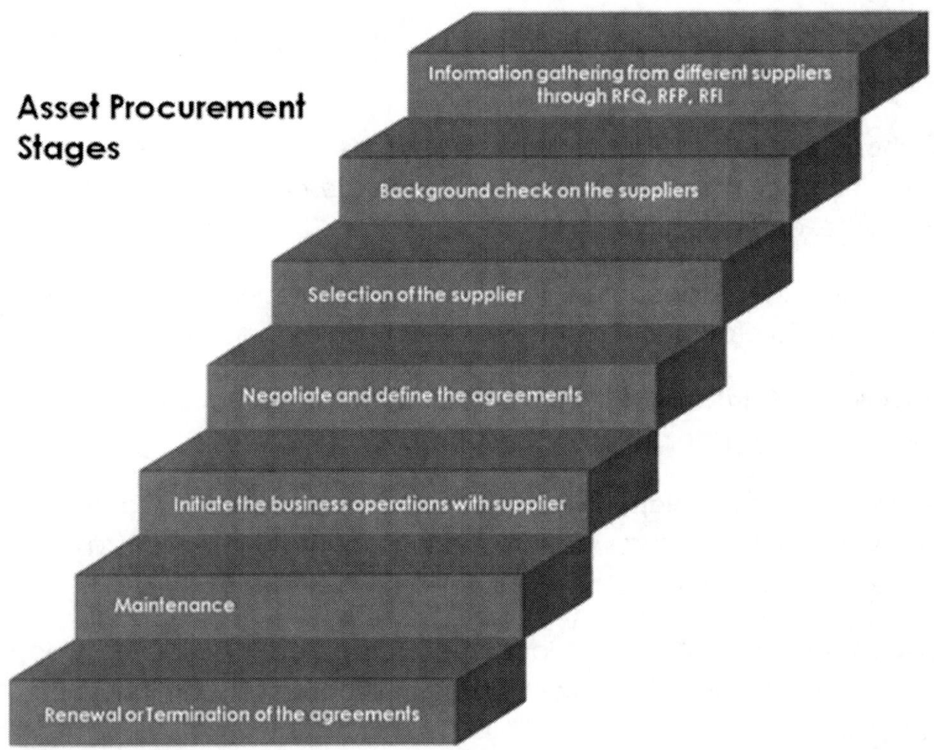

1. Information gathering from different suppliers through RFQ, RFP, RFI.

2. Background check on the suppliers
3. Selection of the supplier
4. Negotiate and define the agreements
5. Initiate the business operations with the supplier
6. Maintenance
7. Renewal or termination of the agreements

Asset Procurement's work is triggered by a purchase request from an internal department or inventory team in the organization. Asset Procurement checks whether if the asset already exists in asset inventory, and determines procurement for a new asset.

Main deliverables of asset procurement process are:

- Acquisition plan
- Supplier selection criteria
- Supplier contingency plan
- Supplier contract renewal and termination plan
- Supplier policies, terms and conditions

Objectives

1. Procure goods at the best reasonable costs without compromising on quality.
2. Improve negotiating position with vendors
3. Efficient management of internal operations on tendering, bidding, purchasing, receiving, inspection, inventory control, and disposal.
4. Provide an accurate and consolidated view of the assets in inventory.

Steps for implementing Asset Procurement

Prerequisite

- Defined asset strategy

Plan

Prepare the Project Charter consisting of the Business case, Goal statement, Project Plan, and Roles and Responsibilities.

1. Business Case
   Business case should describe the benefits and opportunities of Procurement management considering the following areas:
   a) What are the short term and long term benefits of this project?
   b) Does this new initiative align with other business processes, if anything exists?
   c) What impacts will this new initiative have on other business units and employees? Pros and Cons.
   d) Business needs.
   e) What are the risks and issues involved, what are the dependencies?
   f) Estimations on cost infrastructure assets and other miscellaneous items (hardware, software, people-ware).
2. Goal statement
   Goals should be closely associated with business case prepared. Goals should be SMART (Specific, Measurable, Achievable, Relevant, Time-bound).
   a) What are the critical success factors?
   b) What are the key performance indicators?
   c) What is the time estimated to see the results?
3. Project Interfaces
   Define the boundaries, scope, relationships of the asset procurement.

4. Project Plan

   Project plan should show the timeline and milestones for various activities to establish asset procurement process in place and run the business.

5. Roles and Responsibilities

   Define RACI model for clarity in roles and responsibilities. Identify the roles needed and hire human resources. Primary roles needed for asset procurement can be defined as:

   a) Asset Procurement Lead
   b) Procurement Analyst

Develop

1. Develop the SOW for Asset Procurement process, defining the:
   a) Scope of services/service assets which will be considered by asset procurement.
   b) Services that are out of scope.
   c) Assign appropriate people for the defined roles and responsibilities.
   d) Hardware, Software and tools required.
   e) Costs involved.
2. Define the policies and standards for all procurement internal activities.
3. Develop supplier management plans like:
   a) Escalation process
   b) Supplier contingency plan
   c) Supplier contract renewal and termination procedures
4. Define the templates for documentations like purchase request (PR), request for quotation (RFQ), request for information (RFI), and request for proposal (RFP's).
5. Establish a database for procurement which will track all the details and activities of the asset procurement process.
6. Categorize the suppliers and their respective products.
7. Establish a bidding system, defining the procedure for contacting a list of suppliers and selection.

8. Define and negotiate the contracts, service level agreements (SLA's), and penalization procedures. Key aspects to be considered in negotiation are:
9. Payment frequency and procedure
10. Asset acceptance criterion
11. Contract closure formalities
12. Define a method to submit purchase requests (PR) to the supplier, capturing all the details of the needed asset.
13. Define the conditions and criteria, when a PR should seek approvals from the Procurement lead and IT Asset Manager.
14. Define a team to register, receive, and inspect the assets with respect to the purchase requests submitted.

Check

1. Ensure a check is performed in inventory before a new PR is placed.
2. Ensure purchase requests are placed with accurate and detailed needs.
3. Ensure that the purchase of assets with high costs gets the necessary approvals from the financial lead and procurement lead.
4. Ensure all PR's are fulfilled in time as per the agreements made.
5. Ensure all purchased assets are insured.
6. Regular reviews on all procured assets to validate:
    a) Price (Are you getting the correct price?)
    b) Quality (Are you satisfied with the quality of products?)
    c) Responsiveness (Does your suppliers respond timely as per the changing requirements?)
    d) Delivery (Are you satisfied with the delivery of goods?)
7. Ensure that you also have a list of alternative suppliers' information for unexpected situations.
8. Ensure that the supplier contact list is prepared, detailing the suppliers and their services.
9. Ensure there are no disputes or no concerns from the suppliers.

Act

1. Review the policies and procedures at regular intervals.
2. Review the contracts, SLA's, and penalization documents periodically.
3. Monitor your supplier's performance periodically in terms of cost, quality, delivery, timeliness, etc.
4. Resolve any disputes or legal cases from the suppliers.
5. Perform internal and external audits at regular intervals.
6. Implement "Green initiatives" and perform operations with social responsibility.

Measures

Key Performance Indicators

a) Number of purchase requests made.
b) Number of purchase requests made accurately.
c) Number of purchase requests with discrepancies.
d) Number of unclosed purchase requests.
e) Policy adherence.
f) Number of trainings planned.

Best Practices

a) Alliances with suppliers.
b) Centralized and integrated asset management tool encompassing all the ITAM processes.
c) Trainings for employees on process and technology.
d) Documentation of all lessons learned.
e) Clarity in roles and responsibilities.
f) Buy assets which are refillable, reusable, recyclable, and eco-friendly.

Asset Procurement Workflow

Analysis

Organizations analyze the supplier's information and products/services from references and previous experiences. Organizations analyze and explore business opportunities with the help of documentation like RFI's, RFQ's, RFP's, and RFT's.

Organizations send RFI's for various suppliers to get information about their products and services, and then suppliers send the information in the form of proposals (RFP's).

For low or medium costing services, organizations directly send RFQ's to Suppliers. For high valued services, organizations follow a procedure which is initiated through RFI, followed by Supplier's RFP, and then followed by a tendering process through RFT's.

Verification and Selection

After organizations (seeking specific services) receive the RFT's from various suppliers, they perform a background check on all the suppliers' information, history, standards followed by the supplier, and various other details.

After careful consideration and analysis of all the details, the buying organization evaluates the suppliers on services based on their cost, quality, and history of services and offers the tender to a specific supplier or suppliers.

Initiation and Maintenance

Organization (buyer) initiates the business operations with a supplier by placing orders or purchase requisitions, and procures assets as per defined contracts agreed by both parties.

Procuring assets is initiated by PR (Purchase Requisitions) which contains vital information about the purchase quality, quantity, specifications, price, delivery date, order due date, method of delivery, and PR number.

Maintenance involves tracking the performance of the suppliers based on the feedback received from different stakeholders in ITAM organization.

Mandatory details for purchase requests are:

- Vendor name
- Asset code
- Asset description
- Last purchase price
- Quantity
- Rate
- Amount
- Date ordered
- Date received
- Shipping address
- Discount voucher number
- Total amount

Mandatory details for tracking the performance of suppliers are:

- Vendor's name and Contact name
- Contact number
- Payment method
- Payment terms and Shipping terms
- Contract period

- Number of Service Level Breaches
- Description of service level breaches
- Currency value of the service level breach
- Satisfaction survey rating for a particular month
- Average rating of the Satisfaction surveys

Renewals and Termination

Renewals and termination of the contracts is done based on the agreements time duration and performance of the suppliers.

Renewals of the contracts are done when the buying organization is satisfied with the services of the suppliers, and the contracts are extended for a further time period.

Termination of the contracts is done when the buying organization has any constraints or when it is not satisfied with the services of the suppliers. Termination of the contracts can be done either partially or completely. Termination of a part of the service/services from a supplier is called partial termination. Termination of the entire contract from a supplier is called complete termination.

Mandatory details needed for contract termination are:

- Date and Time
- Supplier name
- Supplier address
- Primary contact name
- Email address
- Contact number
- Reason for termination of contract
- Issued by

Checklist for Asset Procurement

An effective asset procurement team should maintain the following data on its processes and operations:

Management's perspective

a) Do you have defined policies and procedures for the selection of a supplier?
b) Does your procurement follow policies and procedures to qualify and evaluate suppliers to become partners with your organization?
c) Do you perform background verification procedures to check your supplier's credibility?
d) Do you have procurement planning documents created?
e) Do you have a criterion for selecting a supplier?
f) How often do you review your policies and procedures?
g) Are requirements clearly communicated to the suppliers? How do you assess them?
h) Are all tasks and calculations documented during the evaluation process?
i) Do you have policies defined for termination of the contracts with suppliers?
j) Do you have a supplier quality survey?
k) Do you receive reports on the procured assets? (Assets procured in this week and in this month)
l) Do you have the roles and responsibilities clearly defined like a RACI matrix?
m) Is there appropriate segregation of duties in the RACI defined?

Operations perspective

a) Do you follow the defined policies strictly?
b) Do you track the vendor prices before placing a PR?

c) Do you monitor and track your PR's after placing an order to the supplier?
d) Do you have an approved or preferred supplier list?
e) Do you monitor your supplier's performance periodically in terms of quality, delivery, timeliness, etc?
f) Do you have a list of alternative suppliers for the unexpected situations?
g) Do you need any approvals for placing orders with your suppliers?
h) How many discrepancies do you notice in the procured goods?

IT Asset Inventory Management

Introduction to Asset Inventory Management

Terminology

IT inventory: A location that stocks the IT assets of an organization, tracking the details like what assets are stocked, where they are stocked, who owns them, etc.

Asset inspection: Verification and validation performed by the asset handling team to determine the condition of an asset before it is stocked in the inventory.

Asset class: Group of similar assets.

Replenishment: Refilling the required IT assets in inventory to avoid any time lags causing inconvenience to stakeholders or increased waiting time.

Economic Order Quantity: Order that minimizes the costs and avoids space crunch issues in an inventory (for a buyer) by ordering the assets in an economic or correct quantity.

Safety stock: The stock of assets which are stored and kept aside for use in unexpected circumstances.

Reorder Quantity: The quantity of specific assets that should be placed in the next order.

Stock Requisition: An activity initiated by asset inventory and intimating the asset procurement to procure assets.

Stock Issue: An activity initiated by the supplier, informing the buyer about the issued stock of assets.

Stock Return: An activity initiated by the buyer, returning the stocks to the seller and informing about discrepancies in stocks delivered.

Stock Transfer: An activity initiated by the inventory when it transfers the stock of assets or an asset from one department to another.

Asset Identification Label: A label or a tag that will be affixed on an asset like a unique identifier for its identification.

Overview

Asset inventory management defines a standardized process and procedures for stocking and managing the assets. Asset Inventory places the assets in an organized structure which is easily traceable, accessible, controllable, and manageable. This arrangement of assets in the inventory can be done in 3 ways:

1. Alphabetically: In this arrangement, assets are arranged in an alphabetical order with respect to the name of the manufacturer, asset, etc.
2. Numerically: In this arrangement, assets are arranged in a numerical order based on the purchase order sequence or price, etc.
3. Date based: In this arrangement, assets are grouped based on the date of purchase, delivery dates, etc.

Asset Inventory Process works closely with asset procurement and asset catalog processes, as it sends purchase requests to asset procurement and receives constant requests from the asset catalog. Asset Inventory process manages the stock of assets by:

a) Checking with the suppliers on the arrival of ordered assets.
b) Registering assets with unique tags.
c) Categorizing the assets based on type, service date, cost, and location of use.
d) Arrangement of the stocks in an easy accessible way.
e) Optimum utilization of the inventory area.
f) Inspecting the quality of assets delivered by the supplier.
g) Storing the assets in safe places.
h) Managing the quality of assets received.
i) Forecasting the demand and supply of assets.

j) Replenishing the stocks.
k) Movement of assets to the user's premises.
l) Checking if the asset needs any refurbishment.
m) Returning the defective assets to the suppliers.

Asset Inventory acts as a baseline for accurate and complete details of stocked assets for various stakeholders like asset manager, procurement lead, catalog lead, and inventory lead.

Main deliverables of asset inventory process are:

- Asset identification plan
- Asset categorization procedures
- Asset inspection procedures
- Asset allocation procedures

Objectives

a) Provide accurate and consolidated information on the available stocked items in inventory.
b) Stock the assets in an organized and easily accessible way.
c) Efficiently utilize inventory space.
d) Submit stock requisitions on time to procurement.
e) Reduce unnecessary investments on assets.

Steps for implementing Asset Inventory

Prerequisite

- Defined Asset Procurement

Plan

Prepare the Project Charter consisting of the Business case, Goal statement, Project Plan, and Roles and Responsibilities.

1. Business Case
   Business case should describe the benefits and opportunities of inventory management considering the following areas:
   a) What are the short term and long term benefits of this project?
   b) Does this new initiative align with other business processes, if anything exists?
   c) What impacts will this new initiative have on other business units and employees? Pros and Cons.
   d) Are existing assets easily traceable?
   e) What are the risks and issues involved, what are the dependencies?
   f) Estimations on the cost
2. Goal statement
   Goals should be closely associated with the business case prepared. Goals should be SMART (Specific, Measurable, Achievable, Relevant, Time-bound).
   a) What are the critical success factors?
   b) What are the key performance indicators?
   c) What is the time estimated to see the results?
3. Project Interfaces
   Define the boundaries, scope, relationships of the asset inventory.
4. Project Plan

Project plan should show the timeline and milestones for various activities to establish asset inventory.

5. Roles and Responsibilities

   Define RACI model for clarity in roles and responsibilities. Identify the roles needed and hire the human resources. Primary roles needed for asset inventory, can be defined as:

   a) Asset inventory lead
   b) Inventory analyst

Develop

1. Develop the SOW for Asset inventory process, defining the:
   a) Scope of services/service assets which will be considered by asset inventory.
   b) Services that are out of scope.
   c) Assign appropriate people for the defined roles and responsibilities.
   d) Hardware, software, and tools required
   e) Costs involved
2. Establish IMIS (Inventory Management Information System) which will track all the asset details.
3. Define the policies and standards for all inventory activities.
4. Develop the inventory documents like stock requisition, stock transfer receipt, stock return, etc.
5. Define a method to group your assets which enables you to understand the context and to manage them easily.
6. Define a method to track and identify the assets and its attributes:
   a) Record all hardware serial numbers, model numbers, etc.
   b) Record all software names, versions, and editions, etc.
7. Set up an assets handling team to receive and register the assets in IMIS (Inventory Management Information System).
8. Define a procedure for communicating with other teams like financial management and procurement in clearance of the invoices.

9. Define a procedure for the asset handling team to move the assets at the requestor's premises.
10. Define a procedure to reserve and ship the assets requested through the asset catalog.
11. Define a check-in and check-out policy for all assets being moved from inventory to live environment and vice versa.

Check

1. Ensure that a check is performed in inventory before a new stock request is placed.
2. Ensure that all received assets are registered in the Inventory Management Information System (IMIS).
3. Ensure that an asset inspection is carried out on the assets received.
4. Ensure that assets are received as per the details of the purchase request and stock request.
5. Ensure that the details in invoices match with the details purchase requests.
6. Perform periodic checks on all assets to determine if they need any refurbishment.
7. Ensure that damaged or rejected assets are promptly returned to the supplier for credit.
8. Ensure that the stocks are replenished as per the consumption.
9. Perform a periodic check to see if the assets need refurbishment.

Act

1. Review the policies and procedures at regular intervals.
2. Track and store all the inventory documents, invoices, receipts for future references.
3. Develop a condition assessment and rating system.
4. Perform internal and external audits at regular intervals.
5. Implement "Green initiatives" and perform operations with social responsibility.

Measures

Key Performance Indicators

a) On time delivery of assets.
b) Quality of the delivered assets.
c) Delivery defects made by the supplier.
d) Damages made to the assets by the inventory team.
e) Mismatches found in the invoices and stocks delivered.
f) Unclosed purchase requests.
g) Accuracy of information in IMIS.
h) Movement of assets to the users on time.
i) Number of trainings planned.

Best Practices

a) Company owned inventory.
b) Centralized and integrated asset management tool encompassing all the ITAM processes.
c) Usage of technology to identify, track, and manage the movement of assets.
d) Training for employees on process and technology.
e) Documentation of all lessons learned.
f) Clarity in roles and responsibilities.
g) Effective space utilization in inventory.
h) Effective facilities management.

Asset Inventory Workflow

Inspection

Inventory management team verifies the assets externally and internally to see if the assets match the requirements as per the placed purchase orders and inspects the internal quality of the assets delivered by the suppliers.

Inspection also involves other tasks like:

- Replenishment of the assets
- Separation and allocation of the defective assets
- Return of assets to the supplier
- Checking if the operational assets need any refurbishments

Mandatory details needed for inspection stage are:

- Received date and time
- Location Received
- Purchase order/ request number
- Supplier name
- Billing address
- Remarks
- Asset tag number
- Bar code label number
- Warranty expiration
- Manufacturer name
- Make and Model
- Serial number

- Status (In storage, Operational, Just Arrived, Defective, Disposal)
- Ownership
- Last Check in
- Last Check out
- Last used by

Registration and Categorization

Registration and Categorization involves registering the newly arrived assets with unique identifiers or tags and categorizing the assets into different types, status and classes to make it easily accessible and organized.

Mandatory details needed for registration and categorization stage are:

- Received date and time
- Received from
- Asset tag number
- Bar code label number
- Warranty expiration
- Manufacturer name
- Make and Model
- Serial number
- Asset Status (In storage, Operational, Just Arrived, Defective, Disposal)
- Last Check in
- Last Check out
- Last used by
- Asset type (Network Device, Storage Device, Memory, HDD cables, Network Cables, CMOS Battery, etc.)
- Asset class (Hardware, Software, and etc.)
- Storage Area location

Checklist for Asset Inventory

An effective asset inventory team should maintain the following data on its assets:

Management's perspective

a) Do you have inventory planning documents created like inventory plan, quality plan, backup plan, and disaster recovery plan?
b) Do you encounter shortfalls in your asset inventory?
c) Do you maintain surplus of assets in your inventory? What is the associated cost?
d) Do you have obsolete assets in your inventory?
e) How often do you verify your inventory records?
f) Do you have documented policies defined for all asset types?
g) Do you have documented policies for assets check in and check out?
h) Do you have defined procedures for reporting broken or distorted assets received?
i) Is you inventory scalable?
j) Do you have an emergency response team and plan, for handling and managing critical assets in the situations of any unexpected accidents or natural accidents?
k) Do you receive reports on the stocked assets in inventory?
l) Do you have the roles and responsibilities clearly defined like a RACI matrix?
m) Is there appropriate segregation of duties in the RACI defined?

Operations perspective

a) Do you track all hardware manufacturer details, asset serial numbers, asset model numbers and product numbers?
b) Do you track and maintain all hardware warranty documents? Are they stored at a safe place? Do you have copies (hard copy and soft copy) of the warranty documents?

c) Do you track and maintain all insurance documents? Are they stored at a safe place? Do you have copies (hard copy and soft copy) of the insurance documents?
d) Do you track your software assets with manufacturer name, version, and product number, licenses details, etc?
e) Does your software asset have the brief information of its associated/compatible hardware device or asset?
f) Do you track the date of purchase on assets to identify the asset's lifetime?
g) Do you track the condition of all assets like "New", "Used", "In Use", "Refurbished", and "EOL - End of lifetime"?
h) Do you check the assets condition while receiving the assets from the users in production environment?
i) Do you have written procedures for inspecting the assets received?

IT Asset Catalog Management

Introduction to IT Asset Catalog Management

Terminology

Asset catalog: Single source of information for stakeholders which provides the details of currently available assets in the IT infrastructure.

Overview

IT Asset catalog management is a standardized process which defines procedures for managing the asset catalog. IT Asset catalog management ensures that a catalog is created, updated, maintained, and that the asset's information is updated in the catalog (asset catalog contains accurate information on all available assets in the organization's inventory). Assets information is populated into the asset catalog considering the inputs from asset procurement and inventory.

Main deliverables of asset catalog process are:

- Asset catalogs with accurate and updated information.

Objectives

1. Provides an accurate and updated view of current assets that are available.
2. Provides an easy interface, so that stakeholders can view, select & order assets.

Steps for implementing IT Asset Catalog Management

Prerequisite

- Asset Procurement and Asset Inventory

Plan

Prepare the Project Charter consisting of the Business case, Goal statement, Project Plan, Project Scope, and Roles and Responsibilities.

1. Business case
   Business case should describe the benefits and opportunities of having asset catalog management, considering the following areas:
   a) What are the short term benefits and long term benefits of having asset catalog management?
   b) Does this new initiative align with other business processes, if anything exists?
   c) What impacts will this new initiative have on other business units and employees? Pros and Cons.
   d) Should we have an explicit asset catalog management team or should we integrate with other asset management processes?
   e) What are the risks and issues involved, what are the dependencies?
   f) Business needs
   g) Estimations of costs on infrastructure assets (hardware, software, people-ware) and other miscellaneous things.
2. Goal statement
   Goals should be closely associated with business case prepared. Goals should be SMART (Specific, Measurable, Achievable, Relevant, Time-bound).

a) What are the critical success factors?
b) What are the key performance indicators?
c) What is the time estimated to see the results?

3. Project interfaces

Should define the boundaries, scope, relationships of the asset catalog management.

4. Project plan

Project plan should show the timeline and milestones for various activities and run the process.

5. Roles and Responsibilities

Define RACI model for clarity in roles and responsibilities. Identify the roles needed and hire the human resources. Primary roles needed for asset catalog management, can be defined as:

a) Service Catalog Lead
b) Service Catalog Analysts

Develop

1. Develop the SOW for asset catalog management process by defining the:
   a) Scope of IT services which will be considered by asset catalog management.
   b) Identification of services which are out of scope.
   c) Hardware, Software and Catalog management tools required.
   d) Appropriate people for the defined the roles and responsibilities.
   e) Costs Involved.
2. Identify the assets that are available in the inventory and organization.
3. Classify and group the assets into categories (hardware, software, license, data, licenses, etc.) to define an organized structure.
4. Categorize the grouped assets into portfolios. (If necessary)
5. Define policies and standards.
6. Define catalog template and service catalog portal.
7. Populate the assets in the catalog portal capturing the assets details like model, manufacturer, price, quantity, delivery time to

fulfill the request, impact and urgency of the asset (user should be able to select the impact and urgency), etc.

8. Define an approval procedure for ordering assets which involves high costs.
9. Verify the accuracy of the data populated in catalog.
10. Publish the catalog.
11. Define a change procedure for updating and modifying the assets in catalog.
12. Provide training on process and technology aspects (like usage of the catalog tools, etc.).
13. Define metrics.
14. Implement the asset catalog operations

Check

1. Ensure that the asset catalog portal provides accurate information on assets with all relevant details.
2. Ensure that the service catalog portal or repository is imbibed with 5C's (Complete details, Consistent, Concise, Clear, and acts as a Centralized repository).
3. Verify that the details of assets with inventory and asset procurement, before publishing the assets in the catalog.
4. Schedule periodic reviews to identify the discrepancies in asset catalog.

Act

1. Improve the service catalog data consistently using 5S methodology (sort, stabilize, shine, standardize, and sustain), feedback, and suggestions.
2. Awareness and training programs for the IT staff on using the service catalog.

3. Prepare monthly reports (which should include information about the new services populated in service catalog, should also include financial information about the services).

Measures

Key Performance Indicators

a) Number of assets defined in the catalog.
b) Number of assets that exist in organization, but missing in the catalog.
c) Frequency and number of periodic reviews on the asset catalog.
d) Number of discrepancies found in the reviews.
e) Number of changes made to the asset catalog in a month.
f) Ordered catalog requests in "Approval" status for more than a week.

Best Practices

a) The asset catalog should be very easy to understand for the stakeholders.
b) The asset catalog should encompass all the details of assets available in infrastructure.
c) Training sessions and awareness programs on the usage and importance of the asset catalog for the stakeholders.
d) Periodic reviews on asset catalog.
e) Centralized and integrated asset management tool encompassing all the ITAM processes.
f) Documentation of all lessons learned.
g) Clarity in roles and responsibilities.

Checklist for IT Asset Catalog Management

An effective catalog management team should maintain the following data on its operations:

Management's Perspective

a) Do you have policies defined for the maintenance of the asset catalog?
b) Do you conduct training sessions and awareness programs to spread the use of the asset catalog?
c) Do you have the roles and responsibilities clearly defined like a RACI matrix?
d) Is there appropriate segregation of duties in the RACI defined?
e) Do you conduct periodic reviews on the asset catalog as defined?
f) Do you take feedback from the stakeholders before adding new assets into the catalog?
g) Do you have stipulated time defined for the request fulfillment of an asset?
h) Do you track all the requests received in the asset catalog?
i) Do you have defined procedures to validate the necessity of a request made in the asset catalog?

Operation's Perspective

a) Do all your asset requests go through the asset catalog?
b) Are your requests fulfilled as per the defined time?
c) Are you informed about the status of the requests placed in the asset catalog?
d) Does your asset catalog provide complete details of assets with respect to physical assets?

e) Does your asset catalog show images of the physical assets?
f) Is your asset catalog easy to understand and user friendly?

Asset Catalog Workflow

Design

Design for asset catalog management refers to designing the asset catalog portal or database which will hold the details of assets and will be accessible for the users (internal stakeholders) and external stakeholders (Stakeholders place asset requests based on the asset details available in asset catalog database or portal).

Important tasks to be considered in the design phase are:

- Definition of the structure for service the catalog portal or database.
- Definition of the user groups who can access the service catalog portal or database.
- Classification of the assets into different groups or hierarchies or categories.
- Population of the information (of different assets details) in the asset catalog database.

Verification

Populated asset information is verified if it represents the accurate and complete details like price, specifications of an asset, delivery time, etc.

It also involves the periodic review of the asset catalog to maintain data accuracy and integrity. Verification's objective is identifying the discrepancies on asset information (available in the asset catalog) like:

- Removal of asset's information which are no longer available in inventory.
- Removal of asset's information with inaccurate details.

Publish

After the asset information is verified, the catalog is published for stakeholders as per the stakeholders' privileges. Published asset catalog will only be visible for the authorized users and IT staff.

Mandatory details needed for the asset catalog are:

- Asset Details Information (Make, Model, Color Specifications, Primary purpose, etc.)
- Requester name
- Requester contact number
- Requester work location
- Approvals Obtained (Yes/No)
- Justification of the request
- Urgency of the request
- Impact of the request (Number of people needing the asset)
- Cost of the asset
- Date requested
- Quantity

Software License Management

Introduction to Software License Management

Terminology

License: License is the legal agreement that authorizes the user or users to use a proprietary asset/ equipment as per the defined terms and conditions of the asset/equipment manufacturer.

License entitlements: License entitlements define the allocation of license capacity as per the license agreement. It defines the right of use, how an asset has to be used, who can use it, and how many can use it.

User based licensing: Licensing technique which specifies the number of users, type of users, and who can use an asset.

Capacity based licensing: Licensing technique which defines the allocation, installation and distribution of licenses among devices (computers, servers, etc).

License Key: Alphanumeric characters that act as a key, enabling user/users to use the software for a stipulated time period.

Licensed application: An application that requires a license to use.

Evaluation License: A temporary license granted for a very short time to use an asset.

Permanent License: A permanent license granted on an asset without any restrictions on time.

Grace Period: It is the allotted time duration for an asset's usage without a license.

License Server: Central server on the network to store licenses, and can be accessed by the authorized users.

Floating License: Licenses that can be shared by a large number of users or computers on a network, as per the availability.

Node Locked License: Licenses that are locked to a specific hardware machine.

Dongle License: Licenses that are encapsulated in a small device which will be connected to the computer to make a specific application work.

Not for Resale License: Licenses that can be used only by partners and resellers on their premises for specific product demonstration and training purposes. These licenses are not to be sold.

Overview

Software license management defines a standard process for managing the software licenses to enforce and ensure compliances with software licenses as per the defined contracts. Software license management tracks, controls, and manages the license usage as per the defined contracts in an organization ensuring that the organization doesn't buy an excess of licenses (wasting money), doesn't pay penalties and breach the contracts by using the products after the license expiration. Software license management enhances productivity for employees by maintaining integrated software, reducing costs by optimizing licenses, reducing risks by eliminating non compliances and improving software purchase planning & license management.

Software license management activities will be triggered when the asset is planned to be deployed in an operational environment (which actually happens after an order is placed by a requestor for an asset in the Asset Catalog). The License and Entitlements Lead identifies the licenses required to operate the requested asset, checks whether the necessary software or entitlements are available and grants an entitlement, or decides to place a new license request for asset procurement team.

Software license management can be categorized into two important areas as: User based licensing and Capacity based licensing.

User based licensing is implemented based on the number of authorized users (authorized user licensing), concurrent users (concurrent user licensing), shared users (floating license), etc.

Capacity based licensing is implemented based on the number of installations (installation), processor value entitlements (PVU), node locked license, dongle license, etc.

Main deliverables of software license management process are:

- Creation of software and license distribution plan
- Tracking of software license agreements and certificates
- Tracking of proof of licenses (POL), certificate of authenticity (COA)

Effective collaboration with inventory management and asset procurement will lead to better management of software licenses.

Objectives

a) Track all shared and stand-alone licenses.
b) Provide accurate information about the stocked licenses and licenses in use.
c) Optimize existing software licenses.
d) Ensure license compliance and efficiency

Steps for implementing Software License Management

Prerequisite

- Asset Inventory

Plan

Prepare the Project Charter consisting of the Business case, Goal statement, Project Plan, Project Scope, and Roles and Responsibilities.

1. Business Case

   Business case should describe the benefits and opportunities of having Software License Management by considering the following areas:

   a) What are the short term benefits and long term benefits of having software license management?
   b) Does this new initiative align with other business processes, if anything exists?
   c) What impacts will this new initiative have on other business units and employees? Pros and Cons.
   d) Should we have an explicit software license management team or should we integrate with other asset management processes?
   e) What are the risks and issues involved, what are the dependencies?
   f) Business needs
   g) Estimations of costs on infrastructure assets (hardware, software, people-ware) and other miscellaneous things.

2. Goal statement

   Goals should be closely associated with the Business case prepared. Goals should be SMART (Specific, Measurable, Achievable, Relevant, Time-bound).

   a) What are the critical success factors?
   b) What are the key performance indicators?
   c) What is the time estimated to see the results?
3. Project Interfaces
   Should define the boundaries, scope, relationships of the software license management.
4. Project Plan
   Project plan should show the timeline and milestones for various activities and run the process.
5. Roles and Responsibilities
   Define RACI model for clarity in roles and responsibilities. Identify the roles needed and hire the human resources. Primary roles needed for software license management can be defined as:
   a) License & Entitlement Lead
   b) License & Entitlement Analysts

Develop

1. Develop the SOW for Software License Management process by defining the:
   a) Scope of IT assets which will be considered by software license management.
   b) Identification of assets which are out of scope.
   c) Hardware, Software and license management tools required.
   d) Appropriate people for the defined the roles and responsibilities.
   e) Costs involved.
2. Identify the asset licenses that are available in the inventory and in operational environment.
3. Classify and group the assets licenses into categories based on license type, agreements, costs, and renewal dates, etc. to define an organized structure.
4. Identify the license life span, and define a mechanism to track the license expiration dates and renewals dates.
5. Define a mechanism to get detailed information on purchased licenses and installed licenses.

6. Define a mechanism to get information on the unauthorized software in the organization.
7. Define a mechanism for tracking the proof of purchase on licenses.
8. Define a mechanism to notify the license expiry details.
9. Identify the technical limitations on licenses.
10. Define a procedure for optimum utilization of licenses especially for instances like transferred licenses.
11. Define policies and procedures for license renewal and maintenance.
12. Define policies and procedures for license entitlements.
13. Develop a procedure for associating the requested assets with its respective software licenses and entitlements.
14. Develop a standard procedure for attributing software license entitlements and software license installations to the requested assets.
15. Define metrics.

Check

1. Perform a check in DSL (Definitive Software Library) for every new license utilization and entitlement.
2. Check for the availability of software licenses before placing a request (in procurement) to buy a new license contract.
3. Check the numbers of entitlements provided on a software license, and review the asset utilization at regular intervals.
4. Ensure that there is an appropriate business justification, and management approval for all software licenses involving high cost.
5. Check the license expiration dates periodically.
6. Check the adherence to the audit clauses mentioned in license agreements.
7. Audit the number of software licenses, contracts, entitlements and usage pool.

Act

1. Purchase new licenses as per changing demands.
2. Check for the issues in licenses and report it to the OEM.
3. Check with the stakeholders and remove or uninstall the software which is not used (Any addition/modification/removal is done through RFC).
4. Send alerts when an unauthorized software installation is detected, thereby ensuring adherence with software compliance rules.
5. Detect illegal and unlicensed software, and alert the license lead.
6. Prepare monthly reports depicting the information on licenses in use, stocked licenses, and issues in licenses.
7. Prepare monthly reports on license entitlements.

Measures

Metrics

a) Number of software licenses in use.
b) Number of unused software licenses.
c) Number of licensed software.
d) Number of unlicensed software.
e) Number of entitlements matched to assets.
f) Number of audits performed on software licenses and software.
g) Number of non-conformances with respect to software licenses in audits.
h) Costs involved in licenses.
i) Number of optimized licenses.
j) Purchased versus installed licenses number.

Best Practices

a) Associate the financial information of software licenses with its inventory details.
b) Organize your software licenses in a centralized repository.
c) Track the proof-of-purchase and purchase records.
d) Track the renewal dates when license renewals have to be renewed
e) Reconcile software licenses against current inventory to detect any under or over license situations.
f) Centralized and integrated asset management tool encompassing all the ITAM processes.
g) Documentation of all lessons learned.
h) Clarity in roles and responsibilities.

Checklist for Software License Management

An effective license management team should maintain the following data on its assets:

Management's perspective

a) Do you have defined policies and standards for all kinds of licenses used?
b) Do you follow any standards on license maintenance?
c) Do you forecast future licensing needs?
d) How do you track the costs involved in licenses?
e) On what basis did you select the license monitoring tool?
f) How often do you perform audits on licenses?
g) Do you have defined procedures for reporting non compliant software licenses found?
h) Do you receive reports on expiring contracts (Contracts expiring this week and month)?
i) Do you have the roles and responsibilities clearly defined like a RACI matrix?
j) Is there appropriate segregation of duties in the RACI defined?

Operations perspective

a) Do you have clear understanding of the license contracts?
b) Do you have clear understanding on license models?
c) How often do you check the utilization of software licenses?
d) How often do you place requests to buy new licenses?
e) Do you manage all your licenses and entitlements in a centralized repository?
f) Do you track license editions and versions?

g) Do you have complete knowledge on your license monitoring tool?
h) Do you encounter any unlicensed software?
i) How do you detect unlicensed software?
j) Do you track your license expiration dates manually or through an automated tool?

Software License Workflow

Analyze

The analyze stage checks the availability of asset licenses (software licenses) before the IT asset is placed in the IT operational environment. License and Entitlement team analyzes and determines the stock of different licenses (Evaluation License, Permanent License, Floating License, Node Locked License, Dongle License, Not for Resale License, etc.) with respect to different assets in the infrastructure and entitles the licenses to specific user/users, machines, etc. They analyze the details of all license types, entitlements, upgrade and downgrade of licenses, management of unallocated software licenses, etc.

If the licenses fall short in number then the License and entitlement lead informs the procurement lead for keeping adequate stock of licenses.

Mandatory details for analysis phase are:

- License type (Evaluation, Permanent, etc.)
- License category (Applications, Database, etc.)
- License status (Active, Inactive, etc.)
- License name
- License version
- Maximum number of users per license
- Maximum number of hardware devices per license
- License purchase date
- License expiry date
- License renewal date
- Vendor name

- Total number of licenses
- Used licenses
- Unused licenses
- Rarely used licenses
- Compliance %

Entitlement

License entitlement enables the users to use a specific asset with the respective license; it enables the users to perform different activities like install, update/modify, and use the software with limited, partial, or full permissions. License and entitlement lead performs the entitlement of software, capturing the details like License purchase order, OEM (Original Equipment Manufacturer) Name, Software type, Version, etc.

Mandatory details for the entitlement phase are:

- License limit
- Activation date
- Update time
- Deactivation date
- Expiration date and time
- Host Id/name
- User name
- License type (individual, volume, OEM, free license, trial license, node locked, named-user license, client access license)
- License period
- License entitlements
- Installations allowed
- License version
- Utilization %

Review

License and entitlement lead performs reviews on different aspects of license maintenance as mentioned below:

a) Checks if additional license purchase is required or licenses have to be uninstalled.
b) Checks the utilization of software licenses.
c) Replenishes licenses in inventory and utilization.
d) Checks if the software licenses are compliant.
e) Perform audits at regular intervals.

Mandatory details for review phase are:

- License name
- License type
- License category
- Installations allowed
- Licensed installations
- Unlicensed installations
- Compliance issues (Critical, Major, Minor)
- Non conformances (Critical, Exceptions, Warnings, Observations)
- When the last compliance review was performed
- Number of Purchased licenses
- Number of unused licenses
- Costs involved in unused licenses
- Number of rarely used licenses
- Costs involved in rarely used licenses
- License agreement expiration dates
- Review performed on date
- Review conducted by
- Review Duration (number of days performed)
- Review performed at locations

IT Asset Operations and Maintenance

Introduction to IT Asset Operations and Maintenance

Terminology

Asset Maintenance Plan: Document which defines the list of maintenance activities for an asset or a specific asset type throughout the lifecycle.

Asset Maintenance Management System (AMMS): Information system which will register, track and store information on all the asset maintenance activities.

Asset Utilization: Percentage of time an asset is in operation at user or customer premises.

Asset Knowledge System: A knowledge base which encompasses all the knowledge, lessons learned, and experiences about all the various organizational assets.

Asset Average Life: Average life time of an asset without even a single failure from the date of deployment.

Request for Maintenance: Any request on assets for performing the maintenance of assets.

Request for asset withdrawal: Request from a user or customer to disassociate an asset and return it to the inventory.

Request for asset movement: Request from a user or customer to move the asset from one location to another.

Request for asset transfer: Request from a user or customer to transfer the asset from one employee to another.

Request for asset repair: Request from a user or customer to perform a repair or refurbish an asset.

Asset Usage Policy: A policy mentioning the guidelines for end users on usage and protection of assets.

Asset Condition: Measure of the health of an asset.

Preventive Maintenance: Maintenance activities that are performed periodically on assets before a failure to prevent any kind of failures.

Reactive Maintenance: Maintenance activities that are performed after the asset breakdown or failure (Reactive Maintenance normally turns out to be a costly affair).

Predictive Maintenance: Maintenance activities that are performed after observing the quality degradation on assets.

Overview

Asset Operations and Maintenance defines a standardized process for the operations and maintenance of assets in an organization. Asset Maintenance manages the routine operations on assets like movement of assets from one inventory to a workplace, refurbishment of the assets, and reassignment back to the inventory.

Asset Operations and Maintenance performs the daily operations and maintenance activities based on the requests made in the asset catalog portals or databases.

Asset Operations and Maintenance tasks are performed at two levels: Proactive and Reactive.

a) Proactive Asset Operations and Maintenance: In proactive maintenance, assets are proactively checked and maintained regularly to avoid any downtime.
b) Reactive Asset Operations and Maintenance: In reactive maintenance, assets are repaired or refurbished when there is a failure.

Asset Operations and Maintenance maintains two important documents: Asset Operations and Maintenance Plan and Asset Operations and Maintenance Costs Document.

a) Asset Operations and Maintenance Plan describes all the operations and maintenance activities associated with different assets.
b) Asset Operations and Maintenance Costs document describes the incurred and incurring costs associated with an asset.

All request created by the users to perform any maintenance tasks are called as Requests for Maintenance (RFM). Request for maintenance can be categorized into 4 types: Request for asset withdrawal, Request for asset movement, Request for asset transfer, and Request for asset repair.

RFAW (Request for Asset Withdrawal)

Requests placed by the users to disassociate an organizational asset and return it back to the inventory are called RFAW. RFAW will be reviewed to determine if the ticket is a valid request and contains all the mandatory details to withdraw an asset. A confirmation is made via a telephone call or through an email; a date and time is scheduled to disassociate the asset from the user's operational environment.

RFAM (Request for Asset Movement)

Requests from a user or customer regarding the movement of assets from one location to another are called RFAM. RFAM will be reviewed to determine if the ticket is a valid request and contains all the mandatory details to move the asset. A confirmation is made via a telephone call or through an email; a date and time is scheduled so that the asset is moved to the correct place as requested by the user.

RFAT (Request for Asset Transfer)

Requests from a user or customer to transfer the asset from one employee to another are called RFAT. RFAT will be reviewed to determine if the ticket is a valid request and contains all the mandatory details for transferring the asset. A confirmation is made via a telephone call or through an email; a date and time is scheduled so that the asset is transferred and allocated to another person giving all the ownership rights.

RFAR (Request for Asset Repair)

Request from a user or customer to perform a repair or refurbish an asset is called RFAR. RFAR will be reviewed to determine if the ticket is a valid request and contains all the mandatory details for repairing or refurbishing the asset. A confirmation is made via a telephone call; a date and time is scheduled to repair or refurbish the asset in a stipulated time.

Main deliverables of asset operations and maintenance process are:

- Standard operating procedures for asset handling.

Objectives

a) Perform operational and maintenance tasks on assets.
b) Prepare, monitor and review the maintenance plan and maintenance cost plan.
c) Register, track, and save all the maintenance requests in AMMS.

Steps for Implementing Asset Operations and Maintenance

Prerequisite

- Asset Inventory

Plan

Prepare the Project Charter consisting of the Business case, Goal statement, Project Plan, Project Scope, and Roles and Responsibilities.

1. Business Case

   Business case should describe the benefits and opportunities of having asset maintenance by considering the following areas:

   a) What are the short term and long term benefits of having asset maintenance?
   b) Does this new initiative align with other business processes if anything exists?
   c) What impacts will this new initiative have on other business units and employees? Pros and Cons.
   d) Should we have an explicit asset maintenance team or should we integrate with other asset management processes?
   e) What are the risks and issues involved and what are the dependencies?
   f) Business needs
   g) Estimations of costs on infrastructure assets (hardware, software, people-ware) and other miscellaneous things.

2. Goal statement

   Goals should be closely associated with the business case prepared. Goals should be SMART (Specific, Measurable, Achievable, Relevant, Time-bound).

   a) What are the critical success factors?

b) What are the key performance indicators?
c) What is the time estimated to see the results?

3. Project Interfaces
   Should define the boundaries, scope, relationships of asset maintenance.
4. Project Plan
   Project plan should show the timeline and milestones for various activities and run the process.
5. Roles and Responsibilities
   Define RACI model for clarity in roles and responsibilities. Identify the roles needed and hire the human resources. Primary roles needed for asset maintenance can be defined as:
   a) Asset Maintenance Lead
   b) Maintenance Analysts

Develop

1. Develop the SOW for Asset Operations and Maintenance process by defining the:
   a) Scope of IT services which will be considered by asset maintenance.
   b) Identification of services which are out of scope.
   c) Hardware, Software and Catalog management tools required.
   d) Appropriate people for the defined the roles and responsibilities.
   e) Costs Involved.
2. Develop Asset Operations and Maintenance Plan and an Asset Operations and Maintenance Cost Document.
3. Develop requisition forms for RFAW, RFAM, and RFAR (Capturing all the important details of a request).
4. Develop a standard procedures for handling RFAW (Request for Asset Withdrawal), RFAM (Request for Asset Movement), and RFAR (Request for Asset Repair).
5. Assign individual teams to perform the RFAW, RFAM, and RFAR tasks.

6. Define and develop Preventive, Predictive and Reactive procedures.
7. Develop a reliability mechanism to assess the condition and rate the assets for operational use.
8. Develop an Asset Knowledge System (AKS) for maintaining all the knowledge articles and experiences on the organizational assets.
9. Define Metrics.

Check

1. Ensure all maintenance tasks will be registered, tracked and saved in the Asset Register to identify and capture the changes made to an asset.
2. Ensure all Requests for Maintenance (RFM) tickets are reviewed and classified as RFAW, RFAM, and RFAR.
3. Ensure that the policies and procedures are followed on all RFAW, RFAM, and RFAR tickets.
4. Ensure that preventive maintenance, predictive maintenance, and reactive maintenance procedures are followed.
5. Schedule periodic reviews, to check the completeness in RFM tickets.
6. Check if the asset needs any repair or refurbishment as a proactive/reactive approach.
7. Check the costs and benefits of rehabilitation versus replacement.
8. Ensure that AKS is used effectively to maintain all the knowledge on assets.
9. Ensure that AKS is maintained through regular backups.

Act

1. Update the Procurement and Inventory team about the asset average lifetime.
2. Update the Procurement and Inventory about asset utilization.

3. Prepare and produce reports on all RFM tickets.
4. Make a track of all experiences and lessons learned in AKS.
5. Perform reactive maintenance and predictive maintenance as per scheduled timelines.
6. Prepare reports on assets issues and failures.
7. Prepare reports on productivity and non productive utilization of assets.
8. Give feedback and communicate the lessons learned with other asset management processes.
9. Get involved in meetings with asset suppliers to discuss asset issues and failures.

Measures

Key Performance Indicators

a) Number of RFAW, RFAM, and RFAR resolved and closed on time.
b) Number of RFAW, RFAM, and RFAR received.
c) Asset average lifecycle.
d) Asset utilization rate.
e) Number of assets breakdown.
f) Time taken to resolve and close RFM tickets.

Best Practices

a) Individual teams for managing RFAW, RFAM, RFAR requests.
b) Implementation of asset management tool which integrates all the asset management processes.
c) Implement 5S mechanism to manage the assets well.
d) Centralized and integrated asset management tool encompassing all the ITAM processes.
e) Documentation of all lessons learned.
f) Clarity in Roles and Responsibilities.

Checklist for IT Asset Operations and Maintenance

An effective asset operations and maintenance team should maintain the following data on its operations:

Management's Perspective

a) Do you have policies and standards defined for all asset operational and maintenance activities?
b) Do you have defined preventive, predictive and reactive maintenance procedures?
c) Do you have defined procedures for reducing the maintenance costs?
d) Do you have defined procedures for the movement and transportation of assets?
e) Do you have the roles and responsibilities clearly defined like a RACI matrix?
f) Is there appropriate segregation of duties in the RACI defined?
g) Do you have defined procedures for reporting broken or ineffective assets received?
h) Do you address the asset failures and issues with the respective suppliers?
i) Do you have policies defined for the assets usage in terms of optimum energy usage?
j) Do you have defined guidelines for effective environmental management?
k) Do you have power consumption policies defined?

Operations Perspective

a) Do you follow the policies and standards defined while performing asset operations and maintenance?

b) Do you follow environmental and safety procedures while performing asset operational and maintenance activities?
c) Do you see improvement in the quality of the supplier's goods?
d) Do you maintain the user manuals for all assets?
e) Do you track the condition of assets? and how often do you do it?
f) Do you track the utilization of assets?
g) Do you set apart the assets which have retired so that they are not mixed with operational assets?
h) Do you have the accurate visibility on all the assets in operations, with details like who is using it, where it is, etc?
i) Do you track the causes of assets failures and issues? And work on them?
j) Do you track the assets energy usage?
k) Do you know the carbon footprints of your office?

Asset Operations and Maintenance Workflow

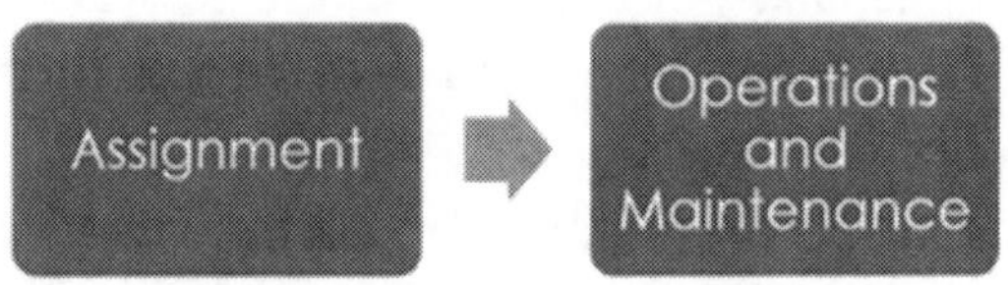

Assignment

Assignment involves segregation of the assets, with its respective licenses to the requested users and business departments as per the respective requests.

Mandatory details needed for assignment and maintenance stage are:

- Assigned date and time
- Assigned to
- Asset tag number
- Bar code label number
- Warranty expiration date
- Manufacturer name
- Model Name and Number
- Serial number
- Asset type (Network Device, Storage Device, Memory, HDD cables, Network Cables, CMOS Battery, etc.)
- Asset class (Hardware, Software, etc.)
- Storage Area location

Operations and Maintenance

Operations and Maintenance involves various operational and maintenance tasks to ensure assets are deployed, updated, changed, removed, and disposed at regular intervals as per the policies defined in ITAM processes. Main activities involved in operations and maintenance are:

a) Accurate regular tracking of asset information like asset owners, asset user, asset location, and other asset attributes like asset tag, serial number, model, manufacturer, etc.
b) Regular internal health checkup of assets and its relevant attributes.
c) Regular identification and categorization of assets which have passed EOL (End of life) period.

Mandatory details needed for assignment and maintenance stage are:

- Asset name
- Manufacturer name
- Model Name and Number
- Serial number
- Bar code label number
- Asset Purpose
- Repair costs
- Warranty expiration date
- Asset Status (In storage, Operational, Just Arrived, Defective, Disposal)
- Last Assigned to
- Asset type (Network Device, Storage Device, Memory, HDD cables, Network Cables, CMOS Battery, etc)
- Storage Area location
- Energy efficiency %
- Carbon credits %

IT Asset Disposal

Introduction to IT Asset Disposal

Terminology

Asset Disposal: Activities or operations necessary to dispose any decommissioned or obsolete asset.

Obsolete Assets: Any asset that no longer serves a purpose or doesn't meet functionality and is out of its warranty period.

Beyond Reasonable Repair: Any asset requiring a repair which will cost the same as buying a new asset.

Asset Disposal Plan: Plan that documents the procedures for disposing an asset and its conditions.

Asset Disposal Criteria: The criterion which defines when an asset has to be disposed from the IT organization.

Asset Disposal Assessment: Assessment made by the asset disposal team to check the condition of an asset and determine whether the asset can be used further or has to be disposed of.

Asset Disposal Approval: The permission granting given by the asset disposal team to dispose of an asset.

Disposal Method: The method which mentions the way on how an asset can be disposed, like reassignment of an asset, resale, donations, scrap, etc.

Data Security Procedure: Procedures that ensure the security of data before the assets are disposed.

Mass Asset Disposal: Disposing large number of assets at a point in time.

Zero Waste: Zero waste is an organizational goal that aims at reusing the assets without sending it to landfills or incineration.

Overview

Asset Disposal process defines and manages the standard procedures for the disposal of retired and obsolete assets as per the organizational, legal, and environmental requirements. Improper asset disposal methods can cause severe fines, lawsuits, and irreparable brand damage.

To avoid any penalties and to mitigate risks involved in the asset disposal process, companies need to proactively define procedures for retiring and disposing of the IT assets, which includes preparing asset disposition policies, standards, and methods.

Asset Disposal Process is triggered when an asset meets the below mentioned asset disposal criteria like:

a) The assets are not required for the organization due to changed business goals and end products.
b) The assets become inefficient to operations.
c) The assets have negative impact on service delivery.
d) The assets become hazardous to use.
e) The assets have met or crossed the expiration date.

Asset Disposal Procedure

Asset disposal procedure is a defined method to dispose an asset in consideration with defined organizational strategies and plans. Asset disposal procedure involves:

a) Identification of assets that meets the asset disposal criteria.
b) Submission of asset disposal form to the Asset Disposal Lead.
c) Perform asset disposal assessment.
d) Approve the asset disposal form.
e) Decide the disposal method.
f) Report the disposal details.

Asset Disposal Methods

Methods for IT Asset disposal can be done based on the asset's functionality, associated financial value, asset utilization, asset average lifetime, and other factors. Some of the well-known methods are:

a) Reassignment to less business critical operations like using in libraries, reception, lobbies, etc.
b) Selling in a public forum.
c) Donations to schools or orphanages.
d) Discarding as scrap after removing the toxic materials considering SHER (Safety, Health, Environment, and Risk) issues.

Main deliverables of asset disposal process are:

- Standard operating procedures for asset disposal.

Objectives

a) Identify the assets which have reached the end of their economic value and are no longer useful for organization.
b) To identify safety, health, environment, risk related issues with assets.
c) To dispose of the assets in the appropriate method based on the associated financial value, asset utilization rate, and asset lifetime.

Steps for Implementing IT Asset Disposal

Prerequisite

- Asset Strategy, Asset Inventory, Asset Maintenance

Plan

Prepare the Project Charter consisting of the Business case, Goal statement, Project Plan, Project Scope, and Roles and Responsibilities.

1. Business Case
   Business case should describe the benefits and opportunities of having asset disposal while considering the following areas:
   a) What are the short term benefits and long term benefits of having asset disposal?
   b) Does this new initiative align with other business processes, if anything exists?
   c) What impacts will this new initiative have on other business units and employees? Pros and Cons.
   d) Should we have an explicit asset disposal team or integrate with other asset management processes?
   e) What are the risks and issues involved, what are the dependencies?
   f) Business needs
   g) Estimations of costs on infrastructure assets (hardware, software, people-ware) and other miscellaneous things.
2. Goal statement
   Goals should be closely associated with the business case prepared. Goals should be SMART (Specific, Measurable, Achievable, Relevant, Time-bound).
   a) What are the critical success factors?
   b) What are the key performance indicators?
   c) What is the time estimated to see the results?

3. Project Interfaces
   Should define the boundaries, scope, relationships of the asset disposal process.
4. Project Plan
   Project plan should show the timeline and milestones for various activities and run the process.
5. Roles and Responsibilities
   Define RACI model for clarity in roles and responsibilities. Identify the roles needed and hire the human resources. Primary roles needed for Asset Disposal can be defined as:
   a) Asset Disposal Lead
   b) Disposal Analysts

Develop

1. Develop the SOW for Asset Disposal process by defining the:
   a) Scope of IT services which will be considered by asset disposal team.
   b) Identification of services which are out of scope.
   c) Hardware and Software required.
   d) Appropriate people for the defined roles and responsibilities.
   e) Costs Involved.
2. Develop an Asset Disposal Plan, Asset Disposal Policy and Zero Waste Goal.
3. Define an asset disposal procedure encompassing identification of assets, assessment of assets, approval, disposal methods, and reporting.
4. Define a status snapshot mechanism for an asset to represent whether if the asset is in "stock", "operational", "repair", and "disposal" statuses.
5. Define data security procedures to protect the confidential data.
6. Develop Request for disposal (RFD) forms capturing the important details of assets.

7. Define asset disposal methods for assets based on the utilization rate, financial value, asset lifetime, assets category, etc.
8. Implement data security procedures on assets before disposal.
9. Define a procedure for mass asset disposal.
10. Define metrics.

Check

1. Ensure that an internal audit happens at regular intervals to determine if assets need to be disposed.
2. Ensure that all asset disposal forms have the mandatory details of assets.
3. Ensure that an assessment is performed on the assets listed for disposal.
4. Determine the residual value.
5. Compare the disposal methods and its associated benefits, costs, and risks.
6. Ensure that all Requests for disposal get approved before they are disposed.
7. Ensure that all the data is wiped off as per the security procedures.
8. Ensure that all the assets to be disposed are tracked and placed in a separate store.

Act

1. Inform the assets details to asset inventory team to delete the disposal assets information from Inventory Management Information system.
2. Inform the asset details to financial management team to segregate the records of disposed assets in the financial management database.
3. Update the finance management team about the estimated revenue generated through asset disposal.

4. Prepare and produce reports on all RFD (Request for Disposal) tickets.
5. Make a track record of all experiences and lessons learned on asset disposal activities.
6. Implement eco-friendly asset disposal operations as per the government and industry regulations.
7. Determine asset values and replacement costs.
8. Keep a record of all the disposed assets.
9. Give feedback and communicate the lessons learned with other asset management processes.
10. Ensure that the asset management takes place in adherence with the zero waste goal.

Measures

Key Performance Indicators

a) Number of RFD tickets received in a month.
b) Number of RFD tickets closed in a month.
c) Number of assets disposed in a year.
d) Revenue generated by assets disposal.
e) Number of audits conducted.
f) Assets waiting for disposal in a store.
g) Number of assets disposed in Mass Asset Disposal.
h) Number of assets disposed as donations.
i) Number of assets sold back to the OEM.

Best Practices

a) Prefer purchasing assets which are refillable, reusable and recyclable.
b) Data must be erased using CESG approved data wiping software. Understand the possible disposal procedures at the time of procuring an asset in association with the supplier.
c) Comply with state and country specific regulations and environmental laws.
d) Store waste equipment with safety precautions.
e) Ensure that all waste goes to an authorized site as per the environment standards.
f) Centralized and integrated asset management tool encompassing all the ITAM processes.
g) Documentation of all lessons learned.
h) Clarity in Roles and Responsibilities.
i) Engage with waste management and recycling companies to dispose and manage the retired assets.

Checklist for IT Asset Disposal

An effective Asset disposal team should maintain the following data on its assets:

Management's perspective

a) Do you have documented policies and procedures for disposing assets?
b) Do you have policies and procedures for waste management?
c) Do you track the revenue generated by disposing the assets?
d) Do you have defined procedures for removing the harmful substances in the assets?
e) Do you receive reports on the disposed assets? (Assets disposed in this month or quarter or year)
f) Do you have a procedure defined for reusing the internal parts of assets?
g) Do you have a procedure for mass asset disposal?
h) Do you have the roles and responsibilities clearly defined like a RACI matrix?
i) Is there appropriate segregation of duties in the RACI defined?

Operations perspective

a) Do you follow policies and procedures for disposing assets?
b) Do you record and calculate the values of asset disposals?
c) How often do you dispose your assets?
d) Do you check the asset condition information and evidences of assets before disposing the assets?
e) Do you set apart the assets which have retired/reached EOL (end of life)?
f) Do you track the type and volumes of assets you are recycling and disposing?

g) Do you have a defined criterion to determine when the asset is at the end of its life cycle?
h) Do you have criteria defined for different types of disposal options?
i) Do you have criteria defined when the internal parts of assets will be reused?
j) Do you remove the harmful substances from the assets such as lead, mercury, bromine, cadmium, etc. from the assets before dumping it as scrap?

Asset Disposal Workflow

Periodic Quality Check

Periodic Quality Checks (PQC) are performed on all the IT assets at regular intervals to check the functionality, reliability, performance, usability, security, safety aspects, and expected EOL (End of life) time period.

Periodic quality checks are performed on all assets that are stocked in inventory to ensure that the IT assets do the intended job in terms of functionality, reliability, performance, usability, security, and safety considerations. It also validates the assets usage and assets maintenance as per compliance, governance, and legal considerations. PQC tracks and reports the issues, risks, and threats based on the condition of IT assets with reference to asset disposal criteria.

Note: A as the IT asset returns back to inventory from the end-user; PQC is performed with reference to asset disposal criteria and asset disposal assessments.

Mandatory details needed for PQC are:

- Asset tag number
- Bar code label number
- Asset type (Network Device, Storage Device, Memory, HDD cables, Network Cables, CMOS Battery, etc)
- Warranty expires on
- Manufacturer name
- Model Name and Number
- Serial number

- Asset Status (In storage, Operational, Just Arrived, Defective, Disposal)
- Last assigned to
- Last PQC performed by
- Last PQC performed date
- Description of the Issues
- Issue Priority
- Description of the Observations

Check for Repair or Replacements

Checking for repair or replacement is done based on the PQC and PQC report on the respective IT assets. Repairing and replacement of an IT asset is based on factors like cost of the asset and complexity involved in repairing or replacing.

If the IT asset is about to pass the EOL time period or has any issues with FURPSS (Functionality, Usability, Reliability, Performance, Security, and Safety), the disposal team makes a decision to refurbish or replace the internal parts of assets. If the IT asset is still under the EOL time period, necessary repairs and replacements are done based on the factors like cost, complexity, and policies.

Mandatory details needed for Check for Repair or Replacement stage are:

- Asset tag number
- Bar code label number
- Asset type (Network Device, Storage Device, Memory, HDD cables, Network Cables, CMOS Battery, etc.)
- Warranty expires on
- Manufacturer name
- Model Name and Number
- Serial number
- Status of an asset (Operational, Repair, Disposal, Retired)
- Last repair performed on date
- Last repair performed by

- Refurbishments parts
- Refurbishments parts make and model

Request for disposal

If the disposal team decides to dispose off an IT asset (Once the IT asset has surpassed the EOL time period or has any issues with FURPSS or it is beyond reasonable repair), they submit a request for disposal (RFD) ticket. Before disposing off any IT asset, the disposal team determines the effectiveness of assets components and sub-components. Then, the team decides whether to dispose off the entire asset or reuse the internal sub-components in any other asset.

Mandatory details needed in Request for disposal stage are:

- RFD number
- Asset tag number
- Bar code label number
- Refurbished part number
- Asset type (Network Device, Storage Device, Memory, HDD cables, Network Cables, CMOS Battery, etc.)
- Warranty expiration date
- Manufacturer name
- Model Name and Number
- Disposal Type (Reassignment to less critical operations, Selling as scrap, Discarding as scrap, etc.)
- Residual value of an asset
- Reason for disposal

Dispose

The disposal team disposes the assets based on FURPSS concerns, financial value associated, asset utilization, asset average lifetime, and other factors. Some of the common disposal methods implemented by organizations are:

- Transfer to less critical operations

  If assets have degraded their functionality, performance, reliability, and usability or when the asset is beyond reasonable repair, the asset disposal team transfers the assets to less critical operations like libraries, reception, lobbies, etc.

- Sale by tender
  Organizations can dispose assets by either internal tender (for internal employees) or external tenders (for general public); they are determined by general attractiveness among internal buyers, external buyers, residual value of the asset, etc.
- Sale by auction
  Assets that are unsuccessful at tenders can be sold in auctions at very low cost.
- Donation
  Assets can also be donated to institutions like orphanages, schools, etc. as per the organizational financial policies and asset disposal policies.
- Cannibalization
  Any assets that are considered as uneconomical proceed with means of cannibalization. Before sending any asset to cannibalization, the asset disposal team removes any reusable components and all toxic materials from the assets as per the government and environmental laws.

Mandatory details needed for the disposal stage are:

- RFD number
- Asset tag number
- Asset description
- Bar code label number
- Asset type (Network Device, Storage Device, Memory, HDD cables, Network Cables, CMOS Battery, etc.)
- Manufacturer name
- Model Name and Number
- Total number of repairs performed
- Method of disposal (Sale by public tender, Reassignment to less critical operations, Selling as scrap, Discarding as scrap, Destroyed, etc.)
- Original cost of the asset
- Residual value of an asset
- Condition Code (Poor, Fair, Good, Excellent)
- Reason for disposal (Archaic, Beyond economic repair, etc.)

- Age of asset

IT Asset Reporting

Introduction to IT Asset Reporting

Terminology

Asset Management Improvement: Strategic initiative for improving the asset management processes and its operations.

Assets Report: Key findings, details, and useful information, on a specific type or group of assets, collated together and presented to the different levels of management and users for making effective decisions and actions.

Asset Summary Report: Summarized information that gives an overall view on organizational assets about the costs, issues, risks, etc.

Requests for Report (RFR): Requests received from any of the stakeholders for asset information in form of reports.

Overview

Asset reporting is a standard process for creating, maintaining, and managing the reports on IT asset management. Asset reporting information will be useful for bringing awareness to the management and improves the management of asset operations.

It defines a systematic approach for handling and managing the Requests for Reports (RFR), gathering the asset information based on RFR requirements, processing the information into reports, and presenting the reports to stakeholders.

Asset reporting produces different types of reports for different levels of management.

a) Reports for Operational Management should be very detailed and contain complete details of every transaction associated with an asset. These reports will generally contain bulky volumes of data, and these reports are normally produced daily.

b) Reports for Tactical Management should have very important details of assets, asset operations, and asset processes; these reports are produced weekly or monthly.
c) Reports for High Level Management should present vital information which should be easily understandable, accessible, and should give a snapshot of the asset operations and processes.

Asset reporting will produce a variety of reports like Informational Reports, Analytical Reports, Compliance Reports, Persuasive Reports, Trend analysis reports, and standard reports (which are ad-hoc, daily, monthly, quarterly and annual).

Important tasks in service reporting are:

a) Data collection
b) Data processing, based on the audience
c) Review
d) Approval
e) Data Publishing and distribution

Data Collection

Data collection is the foundational activity for asset reporting which involves collecting the data about the organizational assets and assets information.

Data Processing

Data processing is the activity which organizes the data into a structure to present the data into organized and useful information.

Data Review

Data review is the activity to verify and validate the data collected and process with respect to the RFR's made by the different stakeholders. Data review is performed technically and editorially.

Data Approval

Data approval is the activity which validates, authorizes, and approves the reports so that they can be sent for distribution.

Data Distribution

Data distribution is the activity which publishes and distributes the data to the requestors.

Main deliverables of asset reporting process are:

- Report templates and reports.

Objectives

a) Provide accurate, useful information on assets to the requestors and stakeholders.
b) Provide consolidated summary on IT asset management.
c) Help the management to make quick and wise decisions with the reports provided.

Steps for implementing IT Asset Reporting

Prerequisite

- Other stabilized asset management processes

Plan

Prepare the Project Charter consisting of the Business case, Goal statement, Project Plan, Project Scope, and Roles and Responsibilities.

1. Business Case
   Business case should describe the benefits and opportunities of having asset reporting by considering the following areas:
   a) What are the short term and long term benefits of having asset reporting?
   b) Does this new initiative align with other business processes, if anything exists?
   c) What impacts will this new initiative have on other business units and employees? Pros and Cons.
   d) Should we have an explicit asset reporting team or should we integrate with other asset management processes?
   e) What are the risks and issues involved, and what are the dependencies?
   f) Business needs
   g) Estimations of costs on infrastructure assets (hardware, software, people-ware) and other miscellaneous things.
2. Goal statement
   Goals should be closely associated with the business case prepared. Goals should be SMART (Specific, Measurable, Achievable, Relevant, Time-bound).
   a) What are the critical success factors?
   b) What are the key performance indicators?
   c) What is the time estimated to see the results?

3. Project Interfaces

   Should define the boundaries, scope, relationships of the asset reporting process.

4. Project Plan

   Project plan should show the timeline and milestones for various activities and run the process.

5. Roles and Responsibilities

   Define RACI model for clarity in roles and responsibilities. Identify the roles needed and hire the human resources. Primary roles needed for asset reporting can be defined as:

   a) Asset Reporting Lead
   b) Reporting Analysts

Develop

1. Develop the SOW for asset reporting process by defining the:
   a) Scope of IT services which will be considered by asset reporting.
   b) Identification of services which are out of scope.
   c) Hardware and Software required.
   d) Appropriate people for the defined the roles and responsibilities.
   e) Costs Involved.
2. Develop an asset reporting plan, asset reporting policy, and standards for creating reports.
3. Selection of appropriate reporting tool.
4. Define a mechanism for stakeholders so that asset report requests can be placed.
5. Define the template for RFR (Request for Report) and capture the most important details needed for generating a report.
6. Develop procedures for manual data collection and automatic data collection.
7. Define a storage location for collected data (where and how the data will be stored).
8. Define the procedure for data processing.

9. Define a procedure for reviewing the report technically and editorially
10. Define an approval procedure before the reports are published and distributed.
11. Define metrics.
12. Define a procedure for storing all the reports generated in a repository.

Check

1. Check the RFR (Request for report) if it's a valid request. Validation is done based on:
   a) The requestor's privilege to access the requested information.
   b) The clarity and completeness of the details in the RFR.
2. Ensure that a technical and editorial review is performed on every report prepared.
3. Ensure that every report has an approval from the Reporting Lead before it gets published and distributed.
4. Ensure that the reports produced meet the needs of stakeholders without any discrepancies.
5. Ensure that the reports are sent only to the requestors at the right time in the appropriate format.
6. Ensure that feedback is collected from the requestors after distributing the reports.

Act

1. Regular periodic evaluation of the reporting process in terms of policies, procedures, and roles and responsibilities.
2. Documentation of lessons learned.
3. Encourage stakeholders to give recommendations and feedback on the reports generated.
4. Store all the reports generated in a repository.

Measures

Key Performance Indicators

a) Number of reports produced for high level management.
b) Number of reports produced for middle level management.
c) Number of reports produced for operational management.
d) Number of informational reports.
e) Number of analytical reports.
f) Number of compliance reports.
g) Number of persuasive reports.
h) Number of trend analysis reports.
i) Number of standard reports.
j) Total number of reports produced in a month.
k) Number of errors in reports.
l) Completeness and Clarity of details in a report.

Best Practices

a) Develop reports for the data which is accurate and complete.
b) Develop reports that measure the right things.
c) Develop reports that are simple and easy to understand.
d) Regular evaluation of reporting process in order to carry out improvements and effectiveness.
e) Centralized and integrated asset management tool encompassing all the ITAM processes.
f) Documentation of all lessons learned.
g) Clarity in Roles and Responsibilities.

Checklist for IT Asset Reporting

An effective asset reporting team should maintain the following data on its operations:

Management's Perspective

a) Do you have defined types and categories for reports?
b) Do you have policies and procedures for creating different types of reports?
c) Do you have any automated tools for creating reports?
d) Do you have defined verification and validation mechanisms for reports generated?
e) Do you have a defined mechanism for collecting feedback on the reports generated?
f) Do you have the roles and responsibilities clearly defined like a RACI matrix?
g) Is there appropriate segregation of duties in the RACI defined?
h) Do you have defined plans for optimum utilization of human resources in the reporting team when there are not many Requests for Reports?

Operation's perspective

a) Do you have defined report templates for different types of audiences?
b) Do you follow the verification and validation procedures before sending reports?
c) How often do you send reports for HLM?
d) How often do you send reports for MLM?
e) How many reports do you send to OLM?
f) Do you receive feedback and recommendations on the reports generated?

g) Do you have defined guidelines to determine the requestors in validating who can receive what?

Asset Reporting Workflow

Data Collection

Data collection is performed through regular checks on IT assets and its information from different ITAM processes.

Data collection focuses on collecting detailed asset information like asset name, asset type, asset class, manufacturer name, location of the asset, cost of the asset, physical specifications of the asset, condition of the asset, etc.

Data collection can also be performed automatically through the usage of automated tools and technology.

Mandatory details for the data collection phase are:

- Asset name
- Manufacturer name
- Location of the asset
- Cost of the asset
- Condition of the asset
- Value of asset
- Issues related with the asset

Data Processing

Data processing is the activity which analyzes and categorizes the RFR's based on priority and the audience who has requested.

Data processing involves collecting data from different ITAM processes, organizing them to make it meaningful, maintaining useful information with an appropriate structure, and performing calculations (if needed, based on the requests).

Data processing also eliminates discrepancies, like redundant RFR's, inconsistencies, and inaccuracies in the drafted reports.

Mandatory details for data processing phase are:

- Asset name
- Asset class (Hardware, Software, Computer hardware, Software licenses)
- Asset type (Service, Facility, Storage, Network, Voice, Batteries, etc.)

Review

Review is the activity to verify and validate the data collected and processed against the report requests made by the different stakeholders. It identifies and evaluates the ability of processed information and determines whether if it fits the business needs. Reviews are performed both technically and editorially.

Approval

Approval is the activity which validates the reports ensuring that the appropriate level of testing and review is performed.

The asset reporting lead takes charge of approving reports before they are published and distributed

Mandatory details for approval phase are:

- Report number
- Report name
- Report type
- Report approved by
- Report created by
- Report requested by

- Report format
- Date created

Publishing & Distribution

Publishing and distribution is the activity which publishes the reports in appropriate formats, fonts, and structures using different tools. It distributes the information to different requestors based on the requests.

Publishing and distribution of the reports can be done in different formats like spreadsheet files, text files, image files, charts, etc.

IT Asset Auditing

Introduction to IT Asset Auditing

Terminology

Audit: An activity for verifying and validating the processes and operations as per their defined policies, plans, procedures, and standards to certify the maturity of organization's operations.

Audit Report: Report produced by the auditor detailing the observations, non-conformances, conformances, best practices observed, risks, recommendations, etc.

Audit Documentation: Documentation that serves as supporting evidence for the auditor to conduct the audit on a specific business function or department.

Overview

Asset Auditing defines an organized approach for performing audits on organizational asset management to ensure that assets are operated, maintained, and managed as per the organizations policies, plans, procedures and standards. It also verifies processes, policies, plans, procedures, and proprietary standards to reduce the chances of risks.

An asset audit helps you to:

a) Build a reliable asset database or register for better decision making
b) Identify the scope of improvements in managing assets
c) Run a business as per regulations and compliances
d) Provides consistency in performing operational activities
e) Reduce the operational and long term risks

Key important activities involved in IT Asset auditing process are:

a) Define the priorities and schedule

b) Definition of audit scope
c) Define an internal team for auditing
d) Perform internal audits
e) Select and appoint an external auditor
f) Prepare for external audit
g) Conduct external audit
h) Report the findings to management

An Auditor from a RCB (Registered Certified Bodies) can perform an external audit to evaluate and certify an organization's specific operations. An auditor evaluates the scope of the audit, identifies the critical and prioritized areas which are very essential for the organization or service provider. An Auditor can adopt different verification mechanisms like inspections, observations, enquiries, computation, and analysis to perform a check on:

a) Process and policies defined
b) Inspection of documents and records
c) Inspection of different databases and repositories like Asset Register, Configuration Management Database, etc.
d) Verification of assets as presented in the balance sheets
e) Checking operations in an operational environment
f) Cross verification with employees and stakeholders

An auditor should be an independent person from a RCB, and who is not:

a) An employee of the organization
b) An employee of the service provider
c) An engineer who assisted in preparing the plans, policies and standards

An auditor should be free from bias, and conflicts of interests towards the organization. He should be honest, truthful, fair, and perform the audit without any discrimination.

Internal Auditor

An inside team or a person of the organization who evaluates the risks, checks and controls the operations as per the defined processes, adds values, elevates the maturity of operations and prepares the organizations for external audits.

External Auditor

An external team or a person from a RCB, who can evaluate and assess the operations of an organization and benchmark the organization's maturity.

Main deliverables of asset auditing process are:

- Internal audit checklists
- External audit checklists

Objectives

a) Capture all asset related information and control the asset operations.
b) Verify and validate the management of assets based on the defined policies, plans, and standards.
c) Ensures that the organization runs its business in accordance with regulations and compliances.
d) To identify the risks and mitigate them before they disrupt the services.
e) To improve and stabilize the asset management operations to a matured level.

Steps for implementing IT Asset Auditing

Prerequisite

- Management support for improving the operations

Plan

Prepare the Project Charter consisting of the Business case, Goal statement, Project Plan, Project Scope, and Roles and Responsibilities.

1. Business Case
   Business case should describe the benefits and opportunities of having asset auditing by considering the following areas:
   a) What are the short term and long term benefits of having asset auditing?
   b) Does this new initiative align with other business processes, if anything exists?
   c) What impacts will this new initiative have on other business units and employees? Pros and Cons.
   d) Should we have an explicit asset auditing team or should we integrate with other asset management processes?
   e) What are the risks and issues involved, and what are the dependencies?
   f) Business needs
   g) Estimations of costs on infrastructure assets (hardware, software, people-ware) and other miscellaneous things.
2. Goal statement
   Goals should be closely associated with the business case prepared. Goals should be SMART (Specific, Measurable, Achievable, Relevant, Time-bound).
   a) What are the critical success factors?
   b) What are the key performance indicators?
   c) What is the time estimated to see the results?

3. Project Interfaces

   Should define the boundaries, scope, relationships of the asset auditing process.
4. Project Plan

   The project plan should, besides showing the timeline and milestones for various activities, run the process.
5. Roles and Responsibilities

   Define RACI model for clarity in roles and responsibilities. Identify the roles needed and hire the human resources. Primary roles needed for asset auditing, can be defined as:
   a) Compliance/Audit Lead
   b) Analysts

Develop

1. Develop the SOW for Asset Auditing process by defining the:
   a) Scope of IT services which will be considered by asset auditing.
   b) Identification of services which are out of scope.
   c) Hardware and Software required.
   d) Appropriate people for the defined the roles and responsibilities.
   e) Costs involved.
2. Develop an asset auditing plan, audit reporting procedures and audit objectives.
3. Develop an internal audit team to evaluate and assess the operations periodically in internal audits.
4. Define the documentation templates and standards for internal audit reports.
5. Define metrics.
6. Select the RCB for performing an audit.
7. Facilitate with necessary artifacts for the auditor to perform an audit.
8. Define a procedure for the internal audit team to work on feedback, recommendations, and non-conformances reported by the auditor.

Check

1. Check the historical information of RCB's before signing the contracts.
2. Perform checks to ensure that all Service owners/Process owners/Leads have relevant knowledge on their respective service, process, or domain to answer the auditor's questions appropriately.
3. Perform internal audits periodically to evaluate and monitor the operations continuously.
4. Ensure that audit reports are sent to the stakeholders with all findings, improvements, and recommendations.
5. Ensure that feedback is collected from the stakeholders.

Act

1. Conduct regular training sessions and awareness programs on compliant operations of the organization.
2. Act on the improvement and non-conformances highlighted in the internal audits.
3. Inform the employees about the purpose and procedures of external audits and information.
4. Act on the non-conformances addressed by the external auditor in the stipulated time.

Measures

Key Performance Indicators

a) Number of conducted audits versus planned audits.
b) Number of audit findings classified into non-conformances, observations, and suggestions for improvement.
c) Number of corrective actions performed after the auditing.
d) Time taken to close and resolve the audit findings.
e) Costs of audits (internal audits and external audits).

Best Practices

a) Documentation of audit procedures and explaining the reason.
b) Documentation of all processes, policies, procedures and standards.
c) Assessment of major risks and critical business processes.
d) Effective audit reports with accuracy, completeness, and clarity.
e) Timely actions based on the audit findings.
f) Management and Stakeholders support for the auditing team.
g) Centralized and integrated asset management tool encompassing all the ITAM processes.
h) Documentation of all lessons learned.
i) Clarity in Roles and Responsibilities.

Checklist for IT Asset Auditing

An effective asset auditing should maintain the following data:

Management's Perspective

a) Do you have an audit plan defined?
b) Do you have the audit scope defined clearly?
c) Do you have the audit objectives documented clearly?
d) Do you maintain the copies of important documents?
e) Do you have policies defined when you can terminate the contracts with suppliers?
f) Do you make a follow up and review on previous audit recommendations?
g) Are your policies in adherence with legal and environmental requirements?
h) Do you have roles and responsibilities clearly defined like a RACI matrix?
i) Is there appropriate segregation of duties in the RACI defined?
j) Do the audits happen in the budget scheduled?

Operation's perspective

a) Do you conduct peer reviews before heading for internal and external audits?
b) Do your audits happen as per the defined time schedule?
c) Do your audits get completed as per the defined time schedule?
d) Do you have training sessions and awareness programs on the best practices?
e) Do you have a rating system defined for the internal audits performed?
f) Do you have defined time allocated for working on non compliances and issues raised?

Asset Auditing Workflow

Plan

In this phase, the management staff and Audit lead develop the strategy, nature, scope of the auditing project with respect to critical assets and normal assets, its objectives, conditions, constraints, time duration of the audit, etc. The planning phase is necessary to ensure that the auditing is conducted in an effective and efficient way.

Main activities involved in planning are:

- Identification of the key stakeholders involved in auditing project.
- Understanding the organizational goals & strategy and IT goals & strategy
- Understanding of priorities, conditions, constraints, and business risks.

Gather

This phase involves participation of auditor who gathers information from a respective department or different departments through observations, interviews, questionnaires, surveys, brainstorming sessions, and informal communications. Also reviews and evaluations are conducted to see if the drafted audit scope, objectives, priorities are in the appropriate direction.

Upon the completion of gathering data and information from information systems, people, and other sources, the auditor then gets an understanding and proposes the idea to perform an audit on a specified date and time.

Execute

This phase focuses on executing the audits as mentioned in the scope with its associated conditions and constraints. Audit execution can be performed as:

Preliminary audit: This is a high level evaluation to determine where the ITAM practice stands as per the defined policies, procedures and compliance regulations.

Initial audit: In the initial audit, a detailed and meticulous review is performed on the complete scope, as per the regulations, standards, and plans. Identified observations, issues, risks, and non-conformances are documented in CAP (Corrective Action Plan).

Certification audit: This audit would certify the ITAM department with an award and certificate of registration.

Report

Reporting is the final phase which delivers the outcomes of the auditing process; these outcomes (in form of reports and information, describing the audit findings, recommendations, improvements, observations, non conformances, risks, etc.) are sent to the IT management staff, internal auditing team, and other requestors.

Mandatory information required for the reporting phase are:

- Report number
- Report created by
- Date and Time
- Primary Contacts
- Department audited
- Checklist Used
- Description of the report (Should define results, observations, non-conformances, risks, and conclusions)

- Priority of observations
- Priority of non-conformances
- Priority of risks
- Remediation plan
- Attachments (in the form of images, spreadsheets, and presentations)

Post audit Review

In this phase, a review is conducted on the final report to discuss the results, observations, non-conformances, strengths, weakness and risks to improve the quality of managing the assets. Post-audit review is intended to ensure that management is addressing or has addressed all recommendations, risks, non conformances, and observations.

Mandatory information required for post audit review are:

- Number of recommendations
- Number of risks
- Number of NC's (Non-conformances)
- Number of observations
- Action on recommendation <A> (Fully implemented, Postponed, Partially implemented, Work in progress)
- Action on recommendation <B> (Fully implemented, Postponed, Partially implemented, Work in progress)
- Action on recommendation <C> (Fully implemented, Postponed, Partially implemented, Work in progress)
- Action on risk <A> (Fully implemented, Postponed, Partially implemented, Work in progress)
- Action on risk <B> (Fully implemented, Postponed, Partially implemented, Work in progress)
- Action on risk <C> (Fully implemented, Postponed, Partially implemented, Work in progress)
- Action on NC <A> (Fully implemented, Postponed, Partially implemented, Work in progress)
- Action on NC <B> (Fully implemented, Postponed, Partially implemented, Work in progress)

- Action on NC <C> (Fully implemented, Postponed, Partially implemented, Work in progress)
- Action on observation <A> (Fully implemented, Postponed, Partially implemented, Work in progress)
- Action on observation <B> (Fully implemented, Postponed, Partially implemented, Work in progress)
- Action on observation <C> (Fully implemented, Postponed, Partially implemented, Work in progress)

IT Asset Management Improvement Initiative

Asset Management Improvement Methods

Asset Management Improvement

Asset management improvement is one of the most important initiatives for the effective and efficient management of assets. It identifies and accumulates the feedback, recommendations, issues and risks from all stakeholders. It prioritizes, estimates the cost, defines the value, schedules and implements the improvement initiatives.

Asset Management improvement initiative is necessary to:

1. Select the assets with good quality while purchasing
2. Reduce unnecessary costs in operations
3. Optimize the resources effectively
4. To improve end user/customer satisfaction

Common methods that can be used for asset management improvement are:

a) 5S
b) PDCA
c) SWOT Analysis
d) Poka-Yoke
e) Kaizen Philosophy

5S (Sort, Stabilize, Shine, Standardize, and Sustain)

5S is a name of workplace method that is first invented in Japan. 5S refers to the Japanese words "seiri", "seiton", "seiso", "seiketsu", and "shitsuke". Later translated into English as 5S, referring to Sort, Stabilize, Shine, Standardize, and Sustain which became a popular organizing and improvement method in organizations. 5S can be used for improving various issues in IT asset management like disordered environment, productivity of assets, and end-user/customer satisfaction.

Sort: This stage involves categorization, prioritization and elimination of unnecessary assets from the workplace.

Stabilize: This stage involves tracking and stocking the frequently used and infrequent assets in appropriate & accessible locations.

Shine: In this stage, the condition of assets is reviewed regularly, and different maintenance procedures are developed and implemented.

Standardize: In this stage a standard procedure is defined to sort, stabilize and shine the assets.

Sustain: In this stage, standard procedures are maintained and improvement initiatives are developed to improve the management of assets.

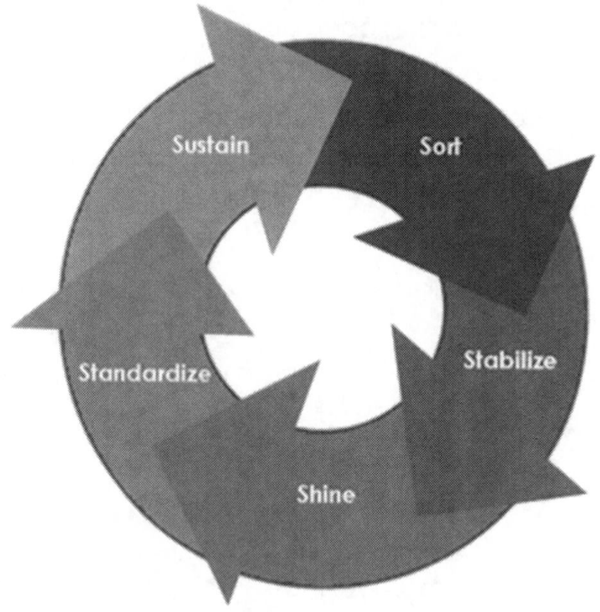

Deming Cycle - PDCA (Plan, Do, Check, Act)

Deming cycle is a methodology for continuous improvement which is also called as PDCA (Plan, Do, Check, Act) approach. This methodology can also be applied in ITAM practice for successful management of IT assets.

Deming cycle is explained by the four phases Plan, Do, Check and Act:

Plan: Prepares series of initial, foundational actions and methodology to be performed for achieving effective management of assets.

Do: Implements the series of actions and activities defined in the Plan phase as per the defined methodology.

Check: Controls the actions ensuring that the activities are implemented correctly and assesses the yielded results with the expected results.

Act: Reviews the actions performed, identifies effective ways of doing things and documents the lessons learned.

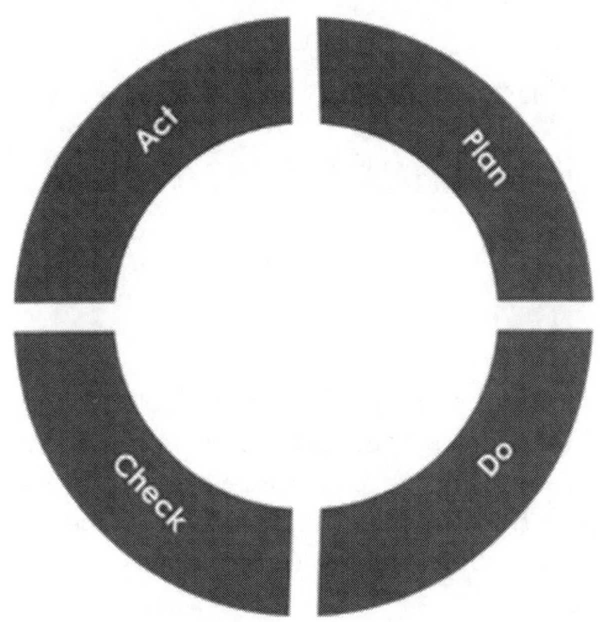

SWOT Analysis

SWOT analysis is another improvement methodology which can be used in ITAM practice for identifying strengths, weaknesses, opportunities, and threats for the management of assets and the policies defined.

For example: SWOT analysis diagram for an organization

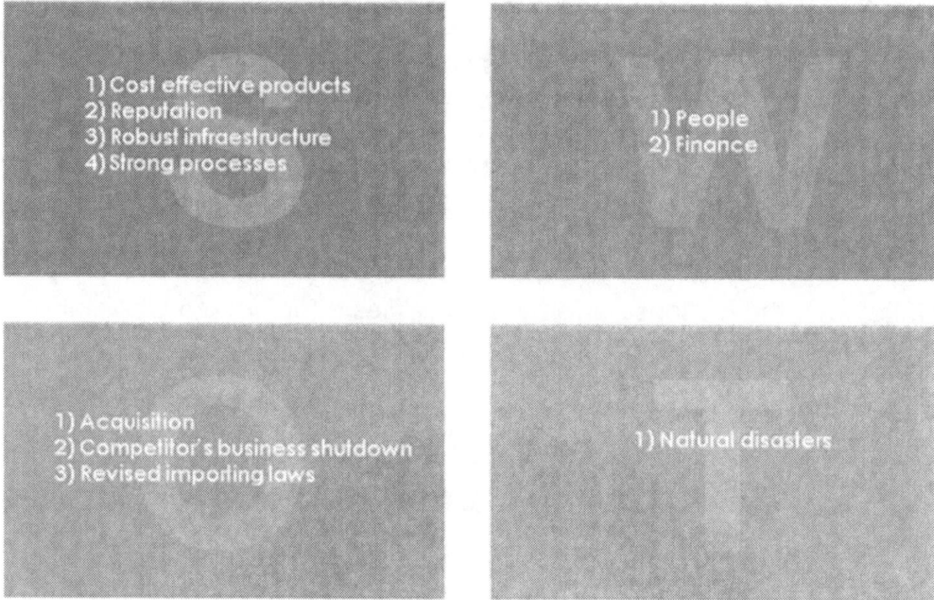

Poka-Yoke

Poka-Yoke is another improvement methodology that can be implemented in ITAM for eliminating defects, non-compliances, and improving effectiveness. The goal of poka-yoke is to prevent errors in the earliest stage and eliminate major failures in the organization. Traditionally poka-yoke defines three approaches as auto-correction, warning, and shutdown.

Auto-correction: With the help of auto-correction method, the business unit will be able to eliminate the chance of errors in ITAM. For example, usage of bar code readers and swiping machines enables us to read the details of assets eliminating confusions or minor errors found in hand written bills or invoices.

Warning: With the help of a warning method, administrators or those with responsible roles in ITAM will be able to get prompt information as warnings in order to take appropriate actions for preventing severe problems. For example, if the users try to install their own software, the system should give an alert to the respective administrators.

Shutdown: With the help of a shutdown method, the system will be shutdown when there is a detection of a threat thereby ensuring that there is no major failure in terms of money, reputation, etc. For example, ITAM applications should be enabled with account lockout or a disabling feature when the user tries to enter the wrong password three times in a row; thereafter, the account should be disabled.

Kaizen Philosophy

Kaizen meaning to break apart, to change, or modify for making things better. Kaizen is another improvement method that can be implemented in asset management for reducing cost, improving quality, and delivery.

Kaizen philosophy eliminates the wastes in the asset management like: Waiting time, Correction of the defects made, Transportation of the assets here and there, Over-production or Over-purchase of assets, Over-processing of the assets, Excess of human resources and Storage place.

Checklist for Improvement initiative

An effective asset management improvement team should maintain the following data on its assets:

a) Do you have a budget allocated for asset management improvement initiatives?
b) Do you have a specific team assigned for improvement initiatives?
c) Do you have specific metrics for measuring the asset management improvements?
d) Do you track and monitor the processes' performance?
e) Do you find inconsistencies and defects in your policies?
f) Do you see the policies being changed as per the recommendations and suggestions provided?
g) How many suggestions/recommendations/improvements do you receive normally?
h) How many suggestions/recommendations/improvements have been implemented?
i) Do you get to see/know the results of reviews, internal audits, and external audits?
j) Do you have a procedure for regular systematic review on all operational procedures for all ITAM processes?
k) Are action plans for improvement developed, documented, and implemented as appropriate?
l) Do you have any system to record customer complaints & feedback, and inputs from employees, suppliers, and other interested parties?

Further Reading

Additional ITAM Processes

Organizations can also define other processes to provide better maturity as per their business needs and priority. Here is a list of other additional ITAM processes which can bring more value and better robustness like: Vendor Management, Asset Security Management, and Risk Management.

Overview of Vendor Management

Vendor management process maintains and manages relationship with vendors/suppliers. Vendor management engages in doing triage for general issues, penalties, and legal issues to maintain an effective relationship with suppliers and partners.

Its main activities involve:

a) Signing a contract with the suppliers and partners.
b) Maintaining the contractual documents and ensuring the asset management operations as per the contractual agreements.
c) Maintain and manage customer relationships by: Raising and discussing issues with the suppliers. Prioritizing and monitoring issues till they are resolved & closed.

Metrics

a) Number of suppliers.
b) Number of lost suppliers.
c) Average delivery time for assets.
d) Number of defective assets per month.
e) Number of escalations, complaints, general issues, legal issues.
f) Number of customer satisfaction surveys sent by vendors.
g) Financial value associated with a supplier

Best Practices

a) Responding to supplier requests on time.
b) Tracking and storing all communications for future references.
c) Establish a vendor improvement plan
d) Getting involved in meetings with the vendors
e) Track the contract dates, rules, regulations, limitations, etc. Make no agreements for long term contracts; make them only for short durations.

Overview of Asset Security Management

Asset Security Management will be a standardized process which develops security policies and procedures, and it ensures to secure and protect the organization's assets preventing any misuse of the organizational assets.

Asset Security Management mainly involves:

- Identification and categorization of assets
- Definition of security policies and procedures
- Implementation of security measures
- Continuous monitoring and improvement

Asset security management also ensures that the assets are safeguarded from any natural disasters.

Metrics:

a) Total number of security policies defined.
b) Number of new security policies created.
c) Number of changes made to policies.
d) Number of security controls implemented.
e) Number of security audit failures.

Best Practices

a) Documented security plans, policies, and processes.
b) Classification and prioritization of IT assets based on the cost, business criticality, etc.
c) Process training sessions and awareness programs.
d) Ensure that security policies and procedures are developed for all asset groups/types/classes.
e) Regular security mock drills to test effectiveness

Overview of Risk Management

Risk Management for assets defines a standardized process which identifies, assesses, prioritizes, and controls the risks on IT assets.

Risks can be defined as any uncertain events that expose the asset to a loss or damage. Risk can be depicted through the formula as "Risk = Probability * Consequence"

Risk management's main objective is the development of risk management strategies, plans, methods, tools and techniques to identify, assess, prioritize and control the risks. Primary activities involved in risk management of IT assets are:

- Identification of critical assets in the organization
- Calculation of the value of assets
- Identification of exposures to losses or damages
- Definition of mitigation plan
- Continuous measurement of risks
- Communication about the issues and risks to different levels of management

Metrics

a) Impact of a risk for a specific asset.
b) Likelihood of a risk for a specific asset.
c) Number of technical risks identified with respect to an asset type.
d) Number of compliance risks identified with respect to an asset type.
e) Number of organizational risks identified with respect to an asset type.

Best Practices

a) Provision of capabilities and resources for effective decision making on threats and opportunities.
b) Encourage proactive risk management (identify opportunities and threats).
c) Adherence to international standards, legal and regulatory requirements.
d) Definition of rapid response teams and emergency response teams.

ITAM Approach for Small Scale Business (SSB)

Normally, small scale businesses cannot afford ITAM consultants or ITAM tools to manage their IT Assets; hence, here are some simple tips highlighted for SSB's.

a) Analyze and understand your asset management operations.
b) Identify the internal factors, external factors, boundaries, and junctions (where your asset management activities integrate with other processes or external factors).
c) Demarcate your asset management operations into simple individual activities.
d) Select the most important asset management processes necessary for your organization. In my opinion, the most important processes for SSB would be Financial Management for IT assets, Asset Procurement and Inventory, and Asset Operations and Maintenance.

   Financial Management for IT assets should be in charge of budgeting, accounting, invoicing, payments and tracking all of these aforementioned aspects.

   Asset Procurement and Inventory should be in charge of procuring, stocking and tracking the assets and their associated licenses.

   Asset Operations and Maintenance should be in charge of tracking, maintaining, delivery, and disposal of assets.
e) Develop ITAM repository
   - Define the policies
   - Collect the data on assets and its attributes from different business units (procurement, human resource, etc.)
   - Organize them into hierarchies/groups
   - Define control procedures
   - Verify the data
   - Keep updating the data
f) Define detailed procedures for all your assets groups.

For example: Guidelines for payments on assets, Guidelines for procuring servers, Guidelines for stocking servers, Guidelines for tracking servers, Guidelines for disposing servers, etc.

g) Define and identify the roles and responsibilities with RACI for all individual activities of asset management operations/systems.
h) Execute the asset management operations.

Primary Roles and Responsibilities in ITAM

IT Asset Manager

IT Asset manager is accountable for the whole asset management practice and its encompassing processes and activities. IT asset manager administers, supports, and manages the contracts for technology spending on IT assets across the organization. The IT asset manager ensures:

- Definition and facilitation of communication between the organization and its suppliers in order to deliver products and services according to plan and within budget.
- Providing advice to management and staff on IT asset management related processes, models, improvements, and best practices.
- Continuous improvemen: on the ITAM-process model framework and alignment with the relevant departments to fine-tune the processes.

Asset Strategy Lead

Asset Strategy Lead is accountable for the strategy management for IT assets process and operations. The strategy lead ensures:

- Definition of process, policies, and standards for defining the strategy.
- Development of the offerings.
- Evaluation of opportunities for business.
- Assessment of opportunities for business with a focus on costs, risks, scope, etc.

Asset Financial Lead

Asset Financial Lead is accountable for the financial management for IT assets process and operations. The financial lead ensures:

- Definition of process, policies, and standards as per business requirements.
- Execution of financial operations (budgeting, accounting, invoicing, and payments) in sync with defined policies.
- Appropriate cash flow management to ensure proper funding with minimal financial charges and in line with business requirements.
- Analysis of opportunities and development of financial models with respect to the strategies defined.

Asset Procurement Lead

Asset Procurement Lead is accountable for the asset procurement process and operations. The procurement lead ensures:

- Definition of process, policies, and standards as per business requirements.
- Execution of the procurement operations (bidding, selection of the suppliers, quoting prices, negotiating the contracts and agreements) in sync with defined policies.
- Developing long term procurement strategy of purchasing materials with visibility and alignment with corporate strategy while considering the continuity of supply with a contingency plan.
- Revenue of bought outs & its associated services as per project schedule on a monthly basis.
- Identification of suppliers, establishment of contracts, cost models and price agreements. It also develops alternate suppliers and solutions.

Asset Inventory Lead

Asset Inventory Lead is accountable for the complete asset inventory process and operations. The inventory lead ensures:

- Definition of process, policies, and standards as per business requirements.
- Execution of the inventory operations (stocking, stock replenishment, stock inspection, and stock returning) in sync with defined policies.
- Reviewing all the purchase requests and purchase orders processed.
- Receiving the goods, physical checking, appropriate storage and maintenance of records.
- Conducting physical count regularly and ensure inventory accuracy.
- Monitoring and reporting of all out of stocks, below safety stocks and expected out of stocks.
- Providing demand shaping recommendations.

Asset Catalog Lead

Asset Catalog Lead is accountable for asset catalog management process and operational tasks. The catalog lead ensures:

- Definition of process, policies, and standards.
- Development and maintenance of the published IT Catalog.

Asset Disposal Lead

Asset Disposal Lead is accountable for asset disposal process and operations. The disposal lead ensures:

- Definition of the process, policies, and standards.
- Retirement and disposal of obsolete assets at the right time in the right way to avoid risks and non-compliances.

- Disposal of garbage in accordance with the waste management plan.
- Risk free asset disposal process including packaging, transportation and warehouse storage.

Assets Audit Lead

Asset Audit Lead is accountable for asset auditing process and operations. The audit lead ensures:

- Definition of the process, policies, and standards.
- Execution of the internal audits and external audits at regular intervals on the defined scope and priorities (to prevent risks and non compliances)as per the business requirements.
- Alignment of internal audit, risk and control activities as per the business strategies.
- Reporting and monitoring the progress of actual audit work performed in relation to the audit plan.
- Leveraging risk mitigation activities and establishing a risk control framework.

Asset Reporting Lead

Asset Reporting Lead is accountable for asset reporting process and operations. The reporting lead ensures:

- Definition of the process, policies, standards, templates and formats.
- Processing, distribution and publication of the reports in sync with the defined process.

Asset Operations Lead

Asset Operations Lead is accountable for asset operations and maintenance process. The operations lead ensures:

- Definition of the process, policies, and standards.
- Execution of the operational and maintenance activities on IT assets.
- Managing asset deployment, administration and installation as per the OEM instructions.

Asset License and Entitlements Lead

Asset License and Entitlements Lead is accountable for the software license management process and operations. Asset license and entitlements lead has the goal to utilize software licenses as efficiently as possible and ensure that the organization is in control of its software licenses. The license lead ensures:

- Definition of the process, policies, and standards.
- Execution of the operational activities like license distribution, administration, control, and renewal of licenses.
- Tracking, evaluating and managing of a wide variety of software licenses and usage.
- Support during audits with respect to software asset licenses.
- Up-to-date knowledge on developments in the market with respect to software license models and entitlements.
- Compliance checking to reconcile license usage to plan for renewals.

Principles for Effective Asset Management

Efficient asset management can be demonstrated with the help of effective processes, clearly defined roles & responsibilities, effective tools, and thorough knowledge on asset information.

Effective processes

1. Should have good integration and alignment with business objectives.
2. Should provide complete guidance for all end to end activities in business operations covering the complete scope, requirements & outcomes.
3. Should provide repeatability that defines the procedure for a system to produce repeatable services/products without any defects.

Effective roles & responsibilities

1. Should define roles for all major tasks & activities.
2. Should demarcate roles and responsibilities by specifying who is responsible, accountable, consulted and informed.

Effective tools

1. Should act as a single point of contact for all asset related information.
2. Should be a single tool for all business requirements and business goals.

Up-to-date knowledge on assets

1. What assets do we have, where are they located, what are the associated costs, and how are they maintained?
2. What is the utilization, and how is the condition of assets measured?
3. How are the imbalances managed like shortage of assets, excess of assets, etc.
4. What are the asset reliability issues, and how are they managed?
5. What are the maintenance costs of assets based on groups or types?

ITAM tool selection

Approach for tool selection

ITAM (IT Asset Management) tools play an important role in effective management of assets as it can:

a) Eliminate routine human work and human errors.
b) Automate the routine tasks.
c) Follow a defined workflow without reinventing the same procedures and approvals.
d) Save time on routine decisions.

Appropriate tool selection for ITAM (IT Asset Management) is a vital task for effective management of assets which will save time, human efforts, and unnecessary costs. Criteria for tool selection should be primarily based on:

a) Organization's Strategy
b) Core functionality
c) Costs and Pricing
d) Organization's infrastructure and architecture
e) Usability and Visualization
f) Technology considerations

Organization's Strategy

Tool selection should be based on Organization's strategy which will be based on:

1. *Organization's goals, objectives, and priorities*
2. *Defined Organizational Policies and IT Policies*

Core functionality

Tool selection should be based on the core functionality of the asset management framework that is:

1. *Business requirements, Functional requirements, and Technical requirements.*
2. *End to end management of asset lifecycle stages.*
3. *Asset management processes needed.*

Costs and Pricing

Tools selection should be based on allocated budget.

1. *Organizations should include the total costs like product cost, licenses costs, support costs, etc.*

Organization's infrastructure and architecture

Tools selection should be based on an organization's infrastructure and architecture by considering:

1. *Organization's Hardware, Software (existing applications and operating systems), People-ware (Employees, Partners and Suppliers)*
2. *Enterprise architecture*

Usability and Visualization

Tools selection should be based on Usability (ease of use) by considering:

a) WYSIWYG feature
b) Searching features
c) Alerting mechanism
d) Data analysis and mining

e) User friendliness
f) Security features

Current technology

Tools selection should be based on the current technology used by considering factors like:

1. *Technology used in other business departments*
2. *Organizations long-term goals using technology like cloud systems, etc.*

Approach for the tool selection for ITAM is explained through Plan, Do, Check and Act Cycle.

Plan

In this phase, management and key stakeholders should understand the goals of the organization, requirements of the ITAM, issues and risks involved. This can be done by performing MoSCoW analysis and SIPOC analysis.

MoSCoW Analysis

MoSCoW stands for Must, Should, Could and Would. It is a method to identify the features, requirements of a tool "What is Must, What is Should, What is Could, and What is would (referring to the future)" to address the ITAM system.

SIPOC analysis

SIPOC is an acronym which stands for Suppliers, Inputs, Process, Outputs, and Customers. SIPOC analysis helps in identifying requirements, issues, risks, and goals of:

- Suppliers (internal suppliers and external suppliers)
- Input sources and input variables
- Processes (sequence of actions) involved
- Outputs, outcomes, and output sinks
- Customers (internal and external)

Develop

In this phase, key stakeholders should consolidate all the ideas and requirements gathered from the Plan phase and contact different ITAM tool providers with the requirements.

This stage involves gathering information from various tool providers about:

- Costs involved
- Core functionality of the product (features provided by the tool with respect to the requirements)
- Support related information
- Compatibility to the organization's infrastructure

Check

In this phase, key stakeholders should check the information gathered on tools from different service providers and evaluate the products by using the trial versions or product demos. Here stakeholders should conduct a SWOT analysis on all the evaluated products and submit a report to management for approval.

SWOT Analysis

SWOT analysis identifies the strengths, weakness, opportunities and threats of the tools evaluated.

Asset Management Process Maturity Framework

AMPMF (Asset Management Process Maturity Framework) can be used to assess the maturity of ITAM business practice.

Maturity for IT Asset Management can be represented using 6 stages as:

1. Chaotic
2. Initial
3. Repeatable
4. Defined
5. Managed
6. Optimized

Chaotic (Stage 0)

Organizations denoting the below mentioned characteristics can be categorized as Chaotic or Stage 0.

- No standard processes, planning documents and policies defined
- Inability to track and monitor the assets accurately
- Unplanned activities (purchasing when necessary, verification performed at times, no budgeting, no proper payments, etc.)
- No dedicated personnel or lacks specific roles and responsibilities for some or all activities
- Struggling to achieve results

Initial (Stage 1)

Organizations denoting the below mentioned characteristics can be categorized as Initial or Stage 1.

- Activities with reactive approach
- Loosely defined roles and responsibilities for all or some activities
- Ability to track and monitor the assets costs and assets information through spreadsheets

Stage 1 mainly relies on processes like Asset Procurement and Asset Inventory.

Repeatable (Stage 2)

Organizations denoting the below mentioned characteristics can be categorized as Repeatable or Stage 2.

- Loosely defined processes, planning documents and policies
- Planned activities with reactive and proactive approach
- Good documentation available with SOP's, Manuals, etc.
- Ability to track and monitor the assets
- Defined quality assurance controls

Stage 2 mainly relies on processes like Strategy generation for IT Assets and Asset Operations and Maintenance.

Defined (Stage 3)

Organizations denoting the below mentioned characteristics can be categorized as Defined or Stage 3.

- Standard processes, planning documents and defined policies
- Ability to track and monitor the assets with a defined asset management tool
- Planned activities with reactive and proactive approach
- Good documentation available with SOP's, Manuals, etc.
- Good awareness among the stakeholders

Stage 3 mainly relies on processes like Strategy generation for IT Assets and Asset Operations and Maintenance and Asset Catalog Management.

Managed (Stage 4)

Organizations denoting the below mentioned characteristics can be categorized as Repeatable or Stage 4.

- Standard processes, planning documents and defined policies
- Ability to track and monitor the assets with a defined asset management tool
- Effective decision making capabilities
- Running the business with care for natural resources and human aspects
- Defined quality assurance controls and regular quality audits

Stage 4 mainly relies on processes like Asset Auditing, Asset Reporting and Asset Disposal.

Optimized (Stage 5)

Organizations denoting the below mentioned characteristics can be categorized as Optimized or Stage 5.

- Ability to track and monitor the assets with a defined asset management tool
- Ability to measure the performance of the ITAM processes
- Integration of ITAM tools and processes with ITSM tools and processes
- Defined quality assurance controls and regular quality audits
- Defined continuous improvement program in place

Stage 5 mainly relies on processes like Asset auditing and Asset management improvement initiatives.

Level	Focus	Asset Management Processes
Stage 0	N/A	N/A
Stage 1	Organized activities	Asset Inventory, Asset Procurement
Stage 2	Repeatability	Asset Inventory, Asset Procurement and Asset Operations and Maintenance
Stage 3	Standardization	Asset Inventory, Asset Procurement, Asset Operations and Maintenance, Software License Management and Asset Catalog Management
Stage 4	Streamlining the asset management	Asset Inventory, Asset Procurement, Asset Operations and Maintenance, Software License Management, Asset Catalog Management, Asset Reporting and Asset Disposal
Stage 5	Optimization	Strategy generation for IT assets, Financial management for IT assets, Asset Inventory, Asset Procurement, Asset Operations and Maintenance, Software License Management, Asset Catalog Management, Asset Reporting, Asset Disposal, Asset Auditing and Asset management improvement initiatives.

Note: This maturity model is just designed as per my knowledge and opinions; it doesn't adhere to any standards or best practices.

Demarcation between ITSM and ITAM

Information Technology Service Management (ITSM) is the provision and management of IT services in an effective and efficient way by providing customer satisfaction to the customers. The term "Service" in ITSM refers to any value creation provided by tangible assets and intangible assets. ITSM can be defined through 5 stages as: Strategy Generation, Service Design, Service Transition, Service Operation, and Continual Service Improvement.

Information Technology Asset Management (ITAM) is the provision and management of IT tangible and physical assets in an effective and efficient way which yields to effective utilization, optimization, and cost reduction for organizations. ITAM can be defined through 3 stages as: Asset Tracking, Asset Control and Asset Optimization.

Similarities in ITSM and ITAM

ITSM is built on 4 pillars: Processes, People, Product/Tools, and Partners (also referred as 4P's of ITSM). ITSM is managed by processes (as defined in ITIL, MOF, etc.), people (through defined roles and responsibilities), products (through tool and technologies used in managing the services) and partners (through good relationship with suppliers, customers, etc.).

ITAM is also built on 4 pillars: Processes, People, Product/Tools, and Partners. ITAM is also managed by processes (as mentioned in this book), people (through defined roles and responsibilities), products (through tool and technologies used in managing the asset lifecycle) and partners (through good relationship with suppliers, customers, etc.).

Dissimilarities in ITSM and ITAM

ITSM is about managing IT Services and IT service lifecycle, efficiently and effectively, to meet the needs of its customers. ITSM ensures:

- Management of IT service lifecycle, right from planning, development, implementation, testing, delivery, support and continuous improvement of service
- Delivery of IT services is continuous, consistent, effective, and are meeting the customer requirements as defined in the agreements.
- Successful alignment of IT services as per the business or customer requirements
- Improvement on the quality of IT services by targeting customer satisfaction
- Providing accurate information on IT services

ITAM is about managing the lifecycle of IT assets, right from purchasing, receiving, stocking, tracking, and disposing the assets. ITAM ensures:

- Providing precise information about the assets (what, where, when, why and how)
- Improvement on the return on investment (ROI)
- Enhanced performance on the utilization of IT assets
- Compliance with hardware and software licensing agreements and other external regulations
- Control on the purchasing, stocking, auditing, and disposal

Demarcation between IT Asset Management and Configuration Management

IT Asset Management is the management of IT assets throughout the lifecycle of assets. It manages asset requisition, asset procurement, asset inventory, asset maintenance, asset reporting, asset disposal, asset auditing, and asset management improvement program. Asset management's main objective is effective tracking, utilization, optimization reduction of the costs and prevention of non compliances in organization.

ITAM deals with 3 types of assets: Hardware, Software, and Licenses & Contracts. ITAM enables in capturing and integrating all three types of assets and their information into a central repository for effective management. But ITAM doesn't depict any relationship between assets and its associated services, nor does it show any impact of changes made on assets.

IT Asset management will be very beneficial to all IT departments irrespective of domains like manufacturing, information technology, aviation, chemical, healthcare, etc.

Configuration Management is the management of configuration items (IT operational assets) in the IT organization which involves installation, identification, tracking the movements, control, verification, and auditing. Configuration management's main objective is to identify and track all the configuration items at one place identifying the dependencies, relationships; also it depicts the impact on other configuration items and its associated services. Configuration management process depicts a comprehensive and consolidated view of the IT operational services.

Configuration Management is considered as the heart of the ITSM processes which encompasses, consolidates, and represents very important information about the configuration items in the IT infrastructure to make effective decisions on effective and efficient service delivery.

Configuration management process work is carried out through 5 sub-processes known as:

- Management and Planning
- Configuration identification
- Configuration control
- Configuration status accounting
- Configuration verification and audit

Configuration management provides great value and help in management of IT services.

Similarities in Configuration Management and IT asset management

Both IT asset management and Configuration management talks about the IT assets.

Dissimilarities in Configuration Management and IT asset management

Configuration management governs the installation, movement, addition and change related activities on Configuration items or live IT assets.

Asset management governs the request fulfillment, procurement, inventory, compliance and disposal activities of IT assets.

Configuration management's main objective is to depict the relationship of configuration items and its associated IT services.

Asset management's main objective is tracking the financial costs, depreciation, return on investment, and optimum utilization of assets.

Configuration management focuses on identifying, tracking, controlling, reporting, and auditing operational IT assets involved in a service.

Asset management focuses on requesting, procuring, stocking, auditing and disposing IT assets.

Appendix

Acronyms

CSF– Critical Success Factors

KPI– Key Performance Indicators

IMAC– Install Move Add Change

ITAM– Information Technology Asset Management

FAR – Fixed Asset Register

FAR – Fixed Asset Reconciliation

GAAP –Generally Accepted Accounting Principles

IFRS - International Financial Reporting Standards

SKU – Stock Keeping Unit

RACI – Roles, Accountability, Consulted, and Informed

PR – Purchase Request

RFQ –Request for Quotation

RFI – Request for Information

RFP–Request for Proposal

EOQ – Economic Order Quantity

IMIS – Inventory Management Information System

NLL – Node Locked License

NFRL– Not for Resale License

AMP – Asset Maintenance Plan

AMMS– Asset Maintenance Management System

AKS – Asset Knowledge System

AAL - Asset Average Life

RFM – Request for Maintenance

RFAD –Request for asset withdrawal

RFAM – Request for asset movement

RFAT – Request for asset transfer

RFAR – Request for asset repair

AUP –Asset Usage Policy

BRR – Beyond Reasonable Repair

ADP –Asset Disposal Plan

ADC – Asset Disposal Criteria

ADA – Asset Disposal Assessment

ADA – Asset Disposal Approval

DSP –Data Security Procedure

AMI –Asset Management Improvement

ASR –Asset Summary Report

RCB – Registered Certified Bodies

NC – Non Conformances

Index